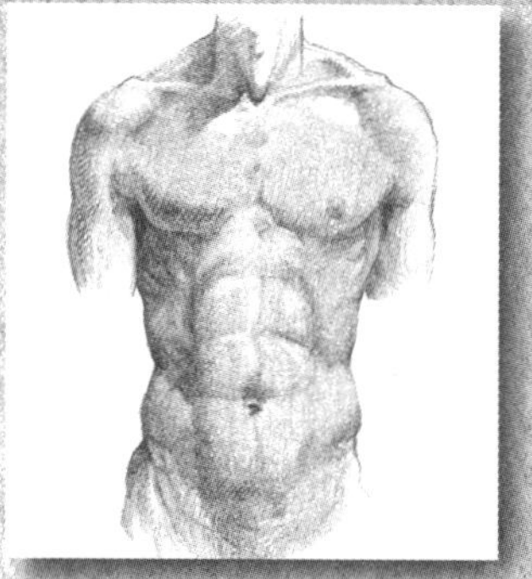

Basic Anatomy
and Figure Drawing

When an artist understands how the human body is composed, it becomes much easier to portray figures accurately and create more realistic renderings. This book introduces the basics of artistic anatomy, focusing on the importance of the skeletal structure and the way muscles cover the bones to create the shapes and forms that we see. Here you'll find information about art materials and how to use them, and you'll also learn to apply your newfound anatomical knowledge to your renderings through illustrated examples and step-by-step drawing lessons. Once you understand the basics, you can develop your artistic anatomy skills by copying from master drawings and photos or sketching from a live model. The more you increase your knowledge and practice your draftsmanship, the more your skills will improve! —*Ken Goldman*

CONTENTS

Choosing Your Materials 2

Practicing Hand Positions 4

Applying Shading 5

Understanding Proportions 6

Getting to Know the Basics 7

Exploring the Torso 8

Depicting the Arm 12

Portraying the Hand 15

Sketching the Leg 16

Drawing the Foot 19

Studying the Head and Skull 20

Capturing Facial Features 23

Portraying a Seated Figure in Pencil 24

Sketching a Standing Figure in Pencil 26

Rendering a Reclining Figure in Charcoal 28

Walter Foster Art Instruction Program 32

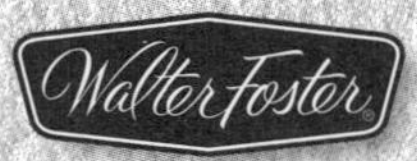

CHOOSING YOUR MATERIALS

With this book, you'll learn more than the names and placements of parts of the body; you'll also learn to render the full form of the figure. Before you begin sketching, take a moment to get familiar with your tools. Only a few materials are needed to begin, and drawing tools are relatively inexpensive, so the initial investment isn't overwhelming. When you're just starting out, however, it's best to purchase the highest quality materials you can afford. Better-quality materials are easier to use and produce more satisfying results; they will ensure that your drawings will last longer and won't fade over time. Here you'll find an overview of the tools you'll need to begin.

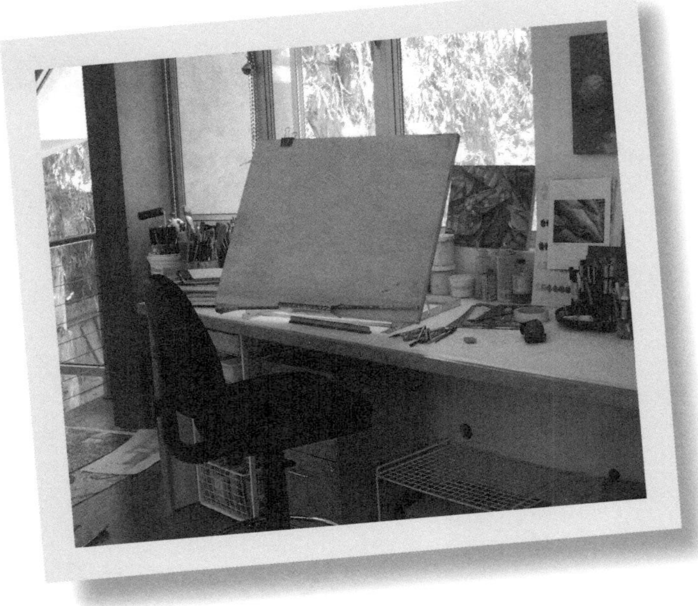

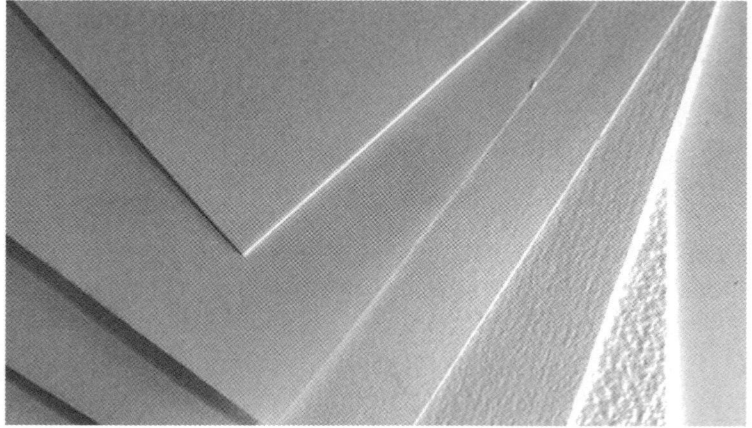

Drawing Papers Single sheets of drawing paper are available in a range of surface textures: smooth grain (plate and hot pressed), medium grain (cold pressed), and rough to very rough. Cold-pressed paper often provides the most versatile drawing surface.

Your Work Station A well-lit, comfortable area will provide the most efficient work environment—you don't need to have a full studio setup to start drawing! Just make sure you have plenty of natural lighting. You'll also need a hard, sturdy work surface and plenty of room to lay out all your tools.

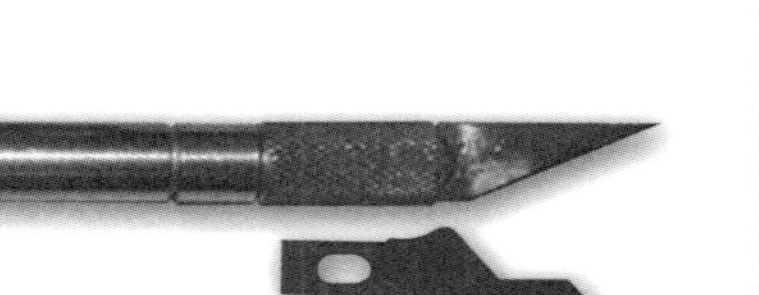

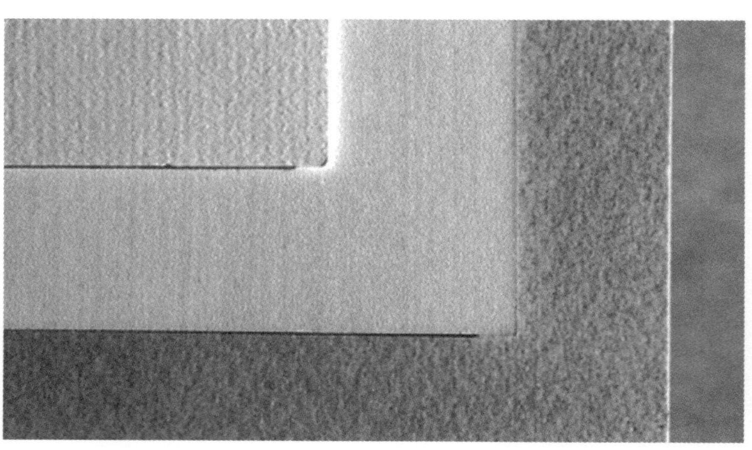

Sharpening Tools Utility knives—or craft knives—come in a variety of shapes and sizes and are great tools for sharpening pencils. You can use them interchangeably with a handheld pencil sharpener and a sandpaper block to alter your points. (See page 3.)

Charcoal Papers Charcoal papers are also available in a variety of textures. They may be used to enhance the texture in your drawings, as their surface finishes can be quite pronounced.

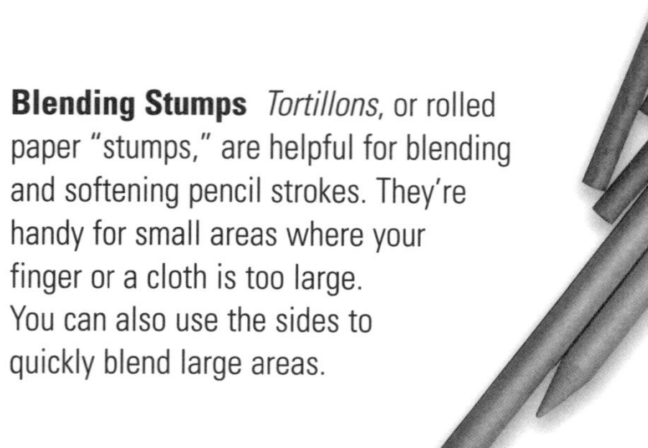

Blending Stumps *Tortillons*, or rolled paper "stumps," are helpful for blending and softening pencil strokes. They're handy for small areas where your finger or a cloth is too large. You can also use the sides to quickly blend large areas.

Erasers A kneaded eraser is an essential tool for creating soft blends and shading. It can be formed into small shapes to "lift out" dark areas to reveal highlights, as well as erase mistakes.

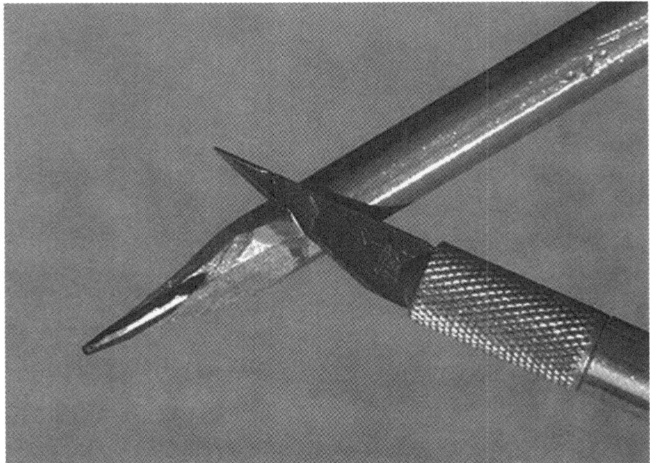

A Knife can create a greater variety of pencil points (flat, blunt, or chiseled) than an ordinary pencil sharpener can. Hold the knife at a slight angle to the pencil shaft, and always sharpen away from you, shaving off only a little wood and graphite at a time.

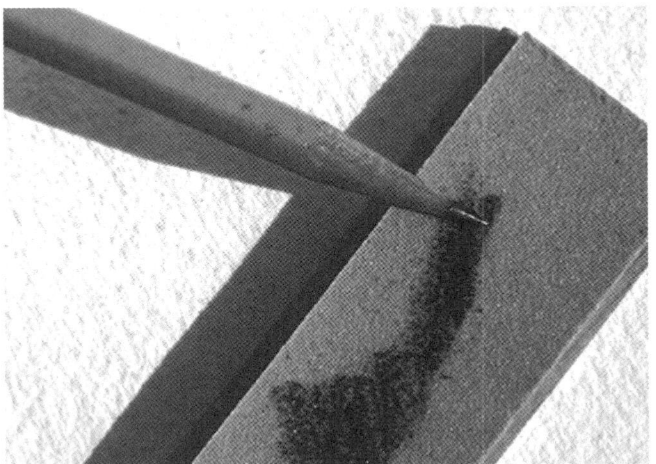

A Sandpaper Block will quickly hone the lead into any shape you wish; it will also sand down some of the wood. To keep the shape even, roll the pencil in your fingers when sharpening.

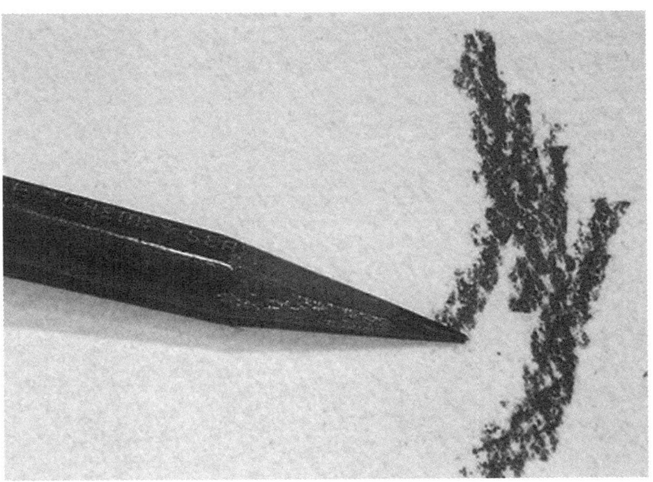

Rough Paper is great for smoothing the pencil point after tapering it with sandpaper. It can also help create a very fine point for small details. Again, gently roll the pencil while honing to sharpen the lead evenly.

Selecting Your Pencils The softness or hardness of the lead (actually graphite) of a pencil is determined by the combination of numbers and letters that are on the pencil's label. Pencils labeled "B" are soft and produce heavy, dark strokes; those labeled "H" have hard lead that creates thin, light lines. HB pencils are in between hard and soft, making them a good beginner's tool. The higher the number that accompanies the letter, the more intense the softness or hardness of the lead. (For example, a 4B pencil is softer than a 2B, and a 4H pencil is harder than a 2H.)

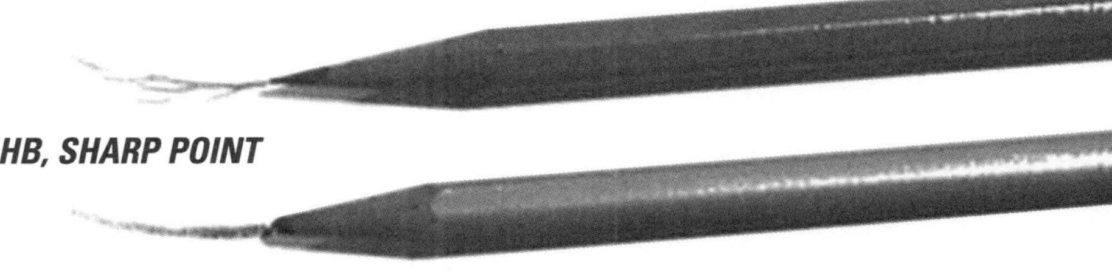

HB, SHARP POINT

HB, ROUND POINT

HB An HB with a sharp point produces crisp lines, and it also allows you to have good control. With a round point, you can make slightly thicker lines and shade small areas.

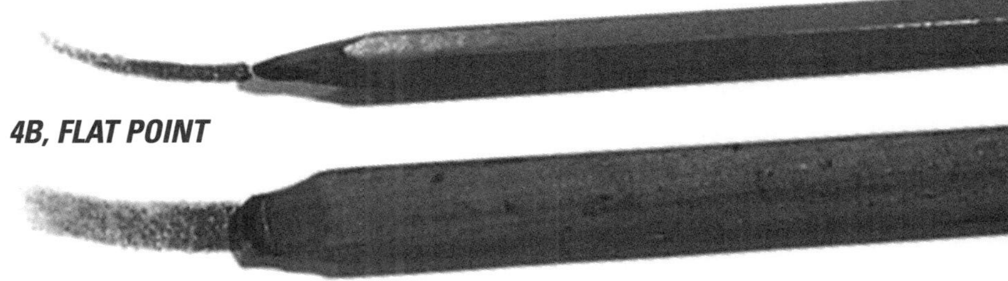

4B, FLAT POINT

FLAT SKETCHING

Flat Use the sharp point of a 4B flat to create wider strokes. A large, flat sketch pencil is good for shading large areas; you can also use the sharp, chiseled edge to create thinner lines.

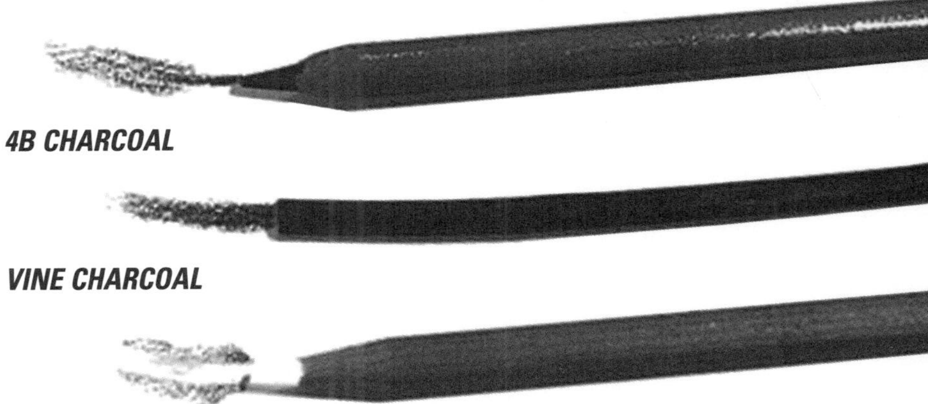

4B CHARCOAL

VINE CHARCOAL

WHITE CHARCOAL

Charcoal 4B charcoal is soft, so it makes a very dark mark. Natural charcoal vines are even softer, and they leave more residue on the paper. White charcoal pencils are good for blending and lightening areas in your drawings.

PRACTICING HAND POSITIONS

The way you hold your pencil will depend on the type of drawing you want
to do. For example, fine detail work is best done with a sharp pencil held as though you were writing, whereas shading
is more easily accomplished with the side of your pencil or a piece of charcoal. As you practice drawing, change hand
positions often and notice the difference this makes in the quality of your lines.

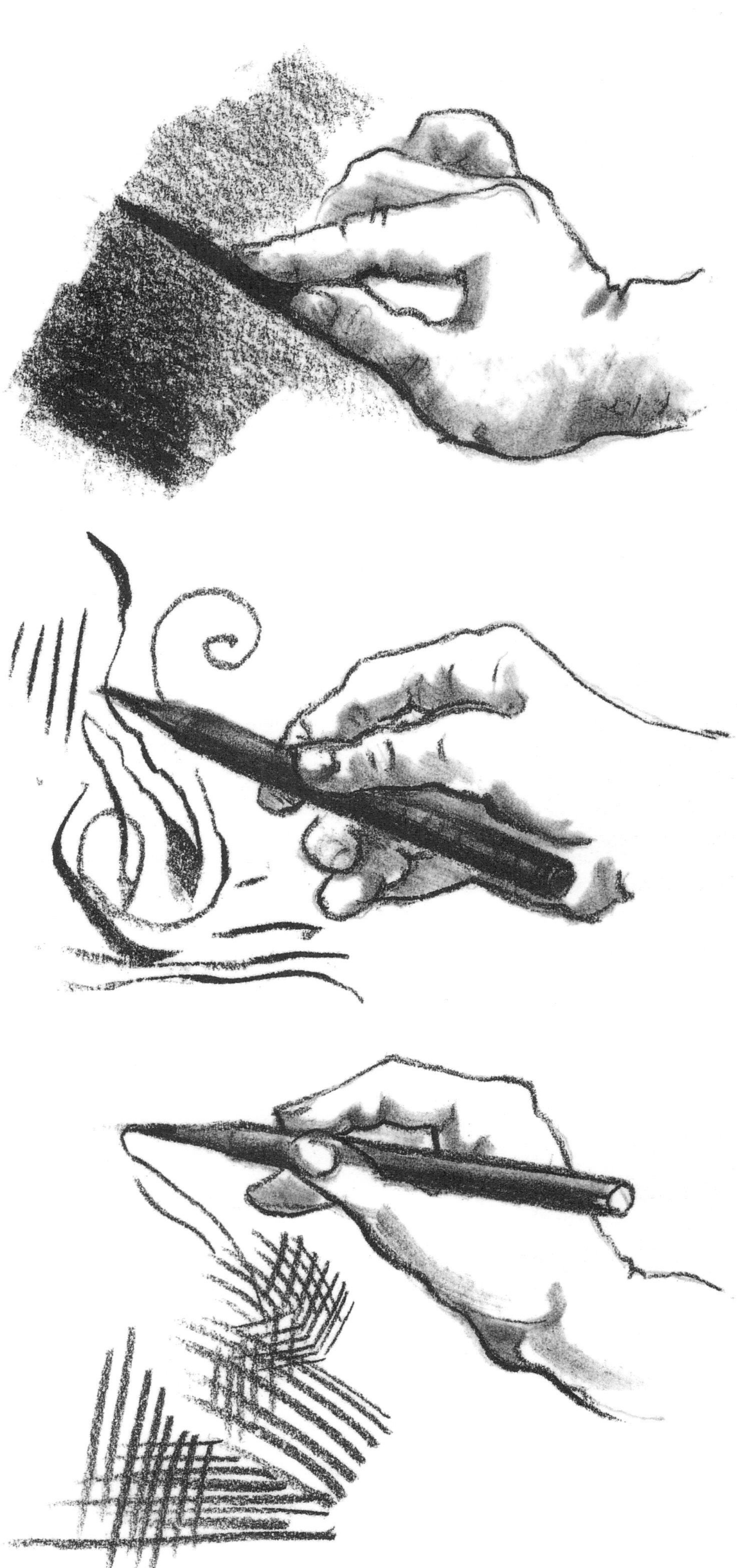

Underhand Position The basic underhand position allows your arm and wrist
to move freely, making it ideal for large,
loose sketches. You can also use this
position with either graphite or charcoal
to create flat strokes, which are essential
for blocking in large areas of shading.

Mid-hand Position The mid-hand
position is good for placing the initial
lines and angles of your drawing. Hold
the pencil lightly and vary the pressure
to create a wide range of expressive
lines. This position produces more precise, detailed strokes than the underhand
position does, but the result is still some-
what loose. The broad, soft lines are
ideal for quick sketches and smaller areas
of loose blocking, shading, or texture.

Handwriting Position The handwriting
position provides the most control, and
the accurate, precise lines that result
are perfect for fine details and accents.
When you use this position, place a clean
sheet of paper under your drawing hand
to prevent your palm from smudging your
drawing. And sharpen your pencils often
to maintain the delicacy of your strokes.

Applying Shading

Artists give a three-dimensional look to a two-dimensional drawing by manipulating values. *Value* refers to the relative lightness or darkness of a color or of black; and it's the variations in value that help define an object's form. Since value tells us even more about a form than its outline, figure artists use a variety of techniques to create a full range of shades and highlights—including the ones demonstrated here; the result is more realistic form and dimension in their drawings.

Flat Shading To shade large areas, create a generalized half-tone by using the underhand position.

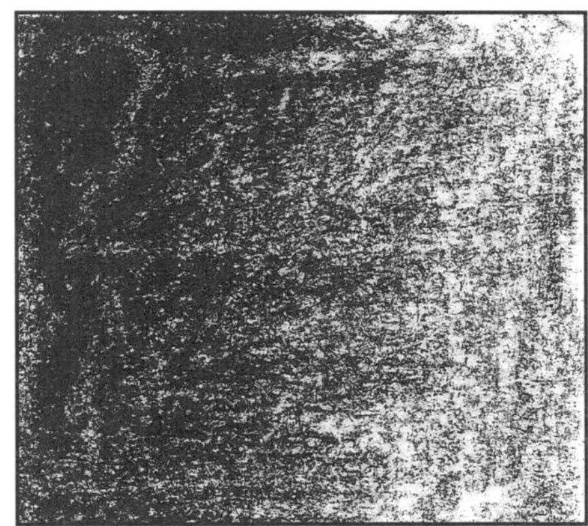

Gradation To produce a gradual shift in value, use the underhand position, varying the pressure from heavy to light.

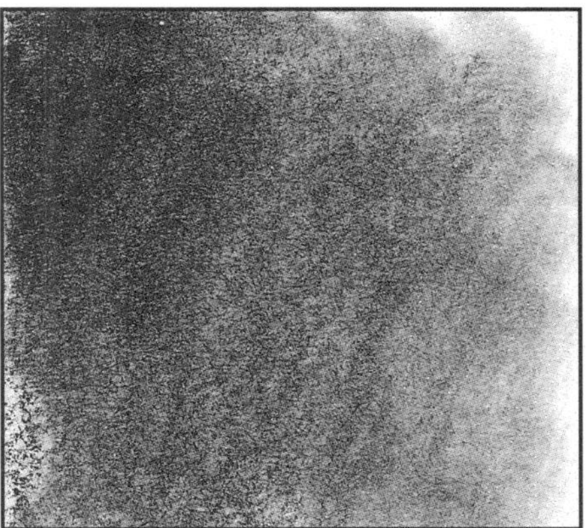

Blending To produce subtle value transitions and soft edges, smudge with your finger or a blending stump.

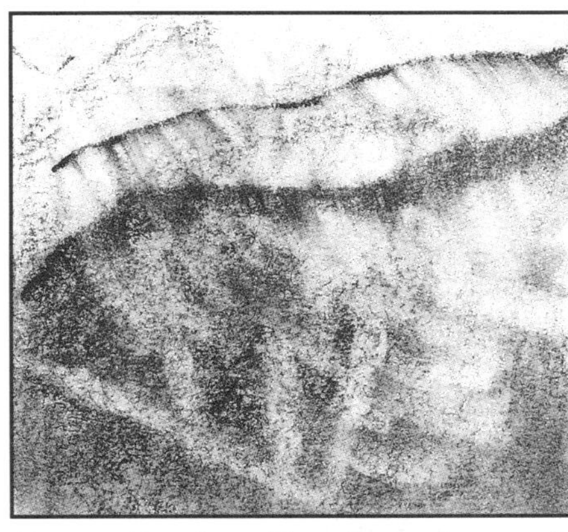

Eraser Strokes To soften edges and vary the line quality, use a small piece of kneaded eraser. (You can also cut off a sharp piece of vinyl eraser.)

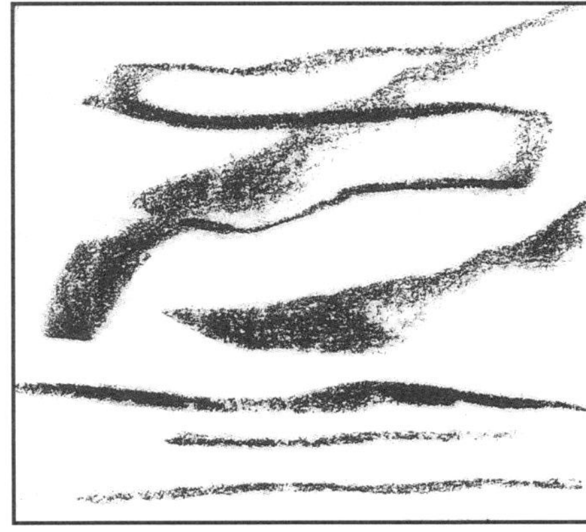

Expressive Lines To draw fluid lines with a dynamic feel, use the mid-hand position; then push, pull, twist, and vary pencil pressure as you draw.

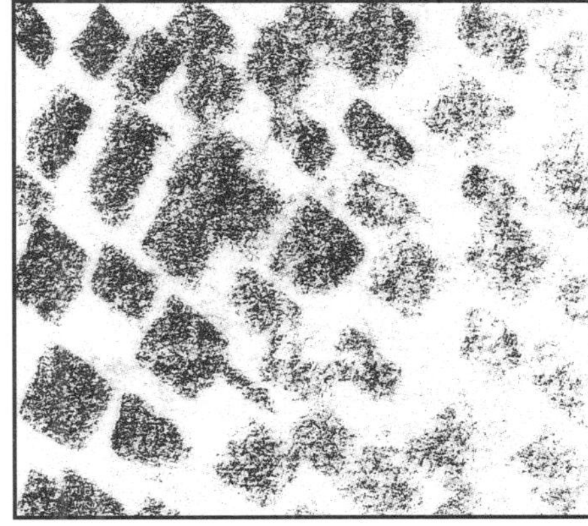

Dotting To create background textures, such as those of a wall or carpet, vary the pressure of your strokes and use your imagination.

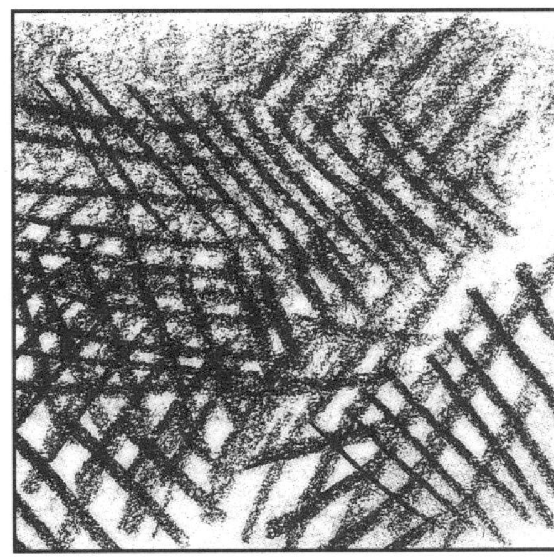

Cross-Hatching To deepen shadows and enhance form, use criss-crossing strokes. The more strokes that overlap one another, the darker the area becomes.

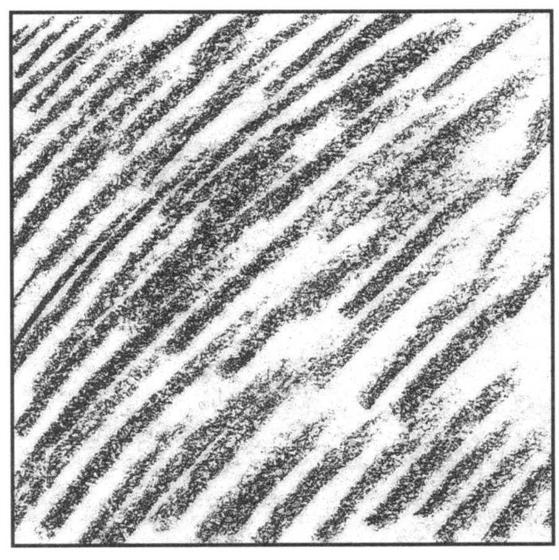

Linear Hatching To create form with shading, make parallel strokes that follow the shape, curve, or direction of the surface. Change the pressure of your strokes to vary the value.

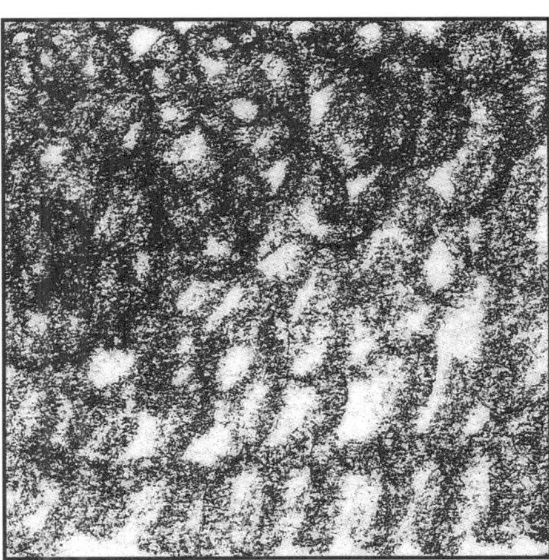

Squiggles For more contrast in your drawings, include loose, circular strokes and squiggles. When used with hatching, these strokes create many interesting textures.

UNDERSTANDING PROPORTIONS

Proportions are an important aspect of figure drawing. *Proportion* is the correct size of one form in relation to another form, such as the size of the head in comparison to the chest. And establishing the correct proportions of a figure before you start developing your drawing is essential for creating realistic renderings. Basic artistic anatomy will provide you with guidelines as to the general proportions that apply to all human figures, but it's also important to note the subtle differences among individual subjects.

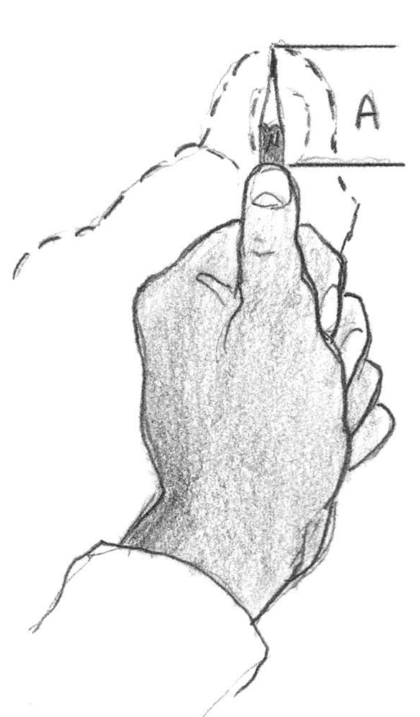

Figure 1

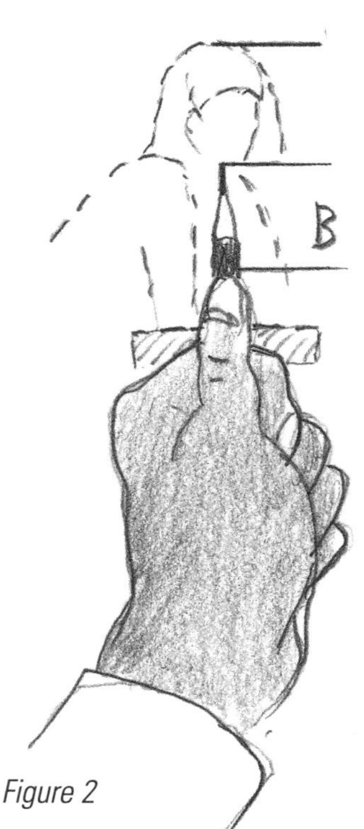

Figure 2

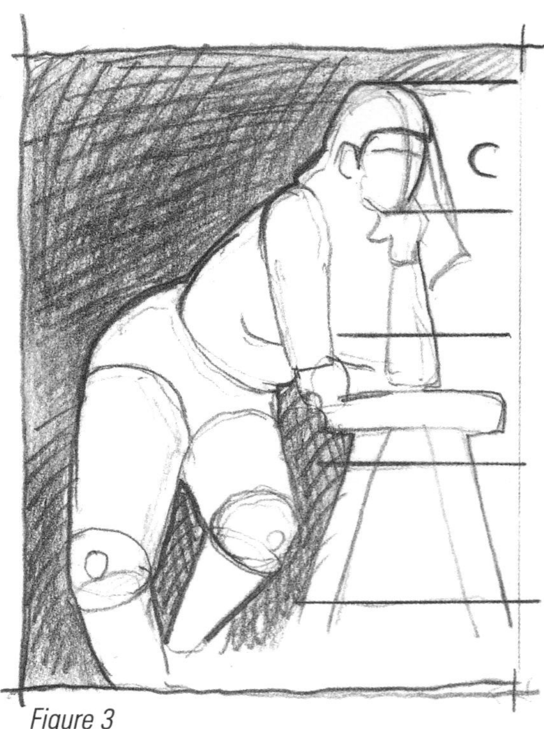

Figure 3

Measuring Proportions To establish general proportions, stretch your arm out straight; visually align your pencil tip with the top of the model's head and align your thumbnail with the chin. (See Figure 1.) This establishes your unit of measurement, 1 head length (A).

Now lower your arm until the tip of the pencil is aligned with the chin. (See Figure 2.) The point where your thumbnail rests is the end of the second head length (B). Continue this procedure until you establish the total number of head lengths that make up the figure.

Use the proportions you've established as a guide (C) as you sketch. (See Figure 3.) To further develop your drawing, simplify complex anatomy by thinking in terms of basic lines and shapes, such as curved lines and cylinders. And fill in the *negative space* (the area surrounding the object) to define the edges of the *positive space* (the model).

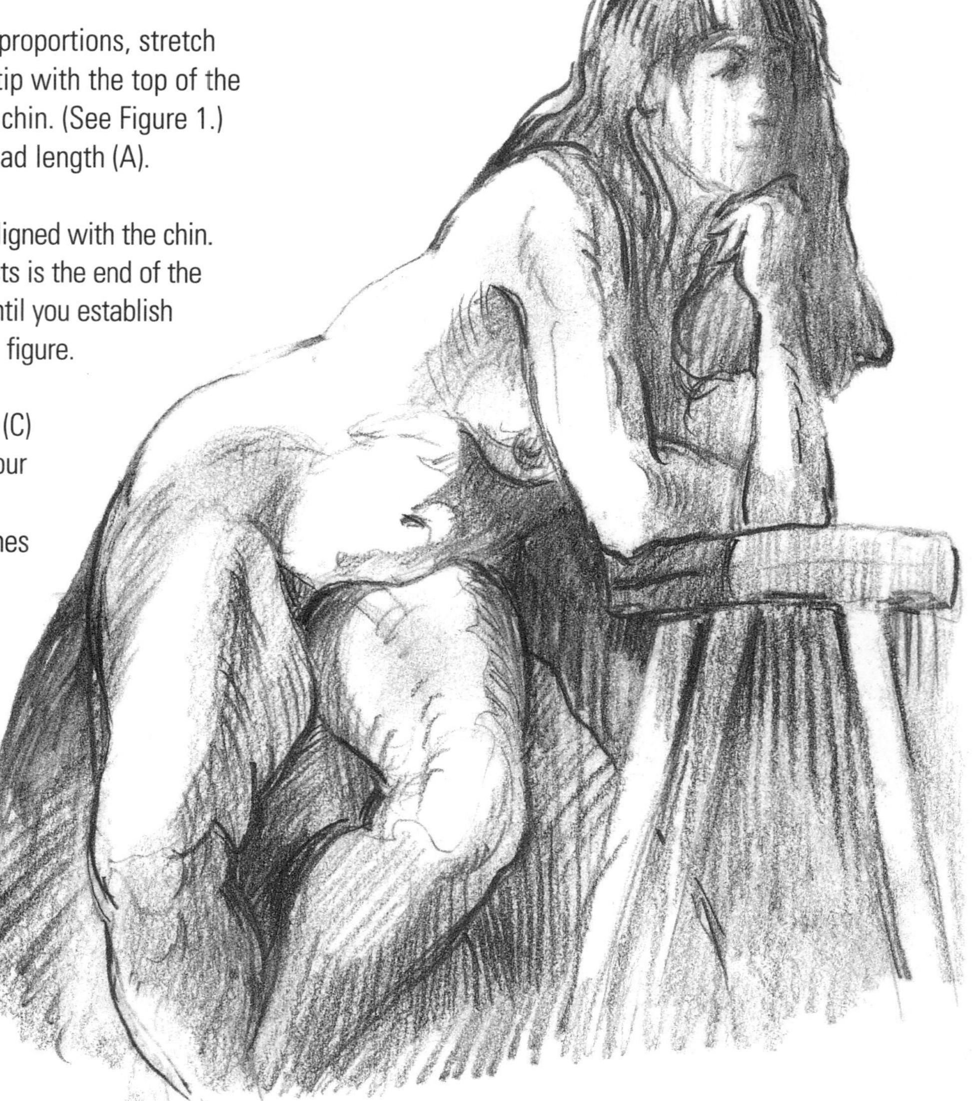

Creating Depth Separating the dark values of the shadows from the light areas of the drawing helps produce a sense of depth and volume. Only a few lines are necessary to show where the edges meet and blend.

Getting to Know the Basics

Now that you're familiar with the fundamental tools and materials needed to begin drawing in pencil, you're ready to move on to the next step. After becoming comfortable with your tools and practicing several different drawing and shading techniques, simply turn the page to get acquainted with the basics of the drawing subject: the human figure.

For many years, leaders in fields as diverse as medicine, science, sports, and art have marveled at the form and function of the human body. In truth, the information an artist needs to know about the body and its basic anatomy has changed little since the time of Leonardo da Vinci. In fact, anatomical drawings made by artists of the 15th century are still in use today! Whereas medical professors and scientists are concerned with the body's function, artists are focused instead on the body's form. *Artistic anatomy*—the focus of this book—explores what creates and influences that form.

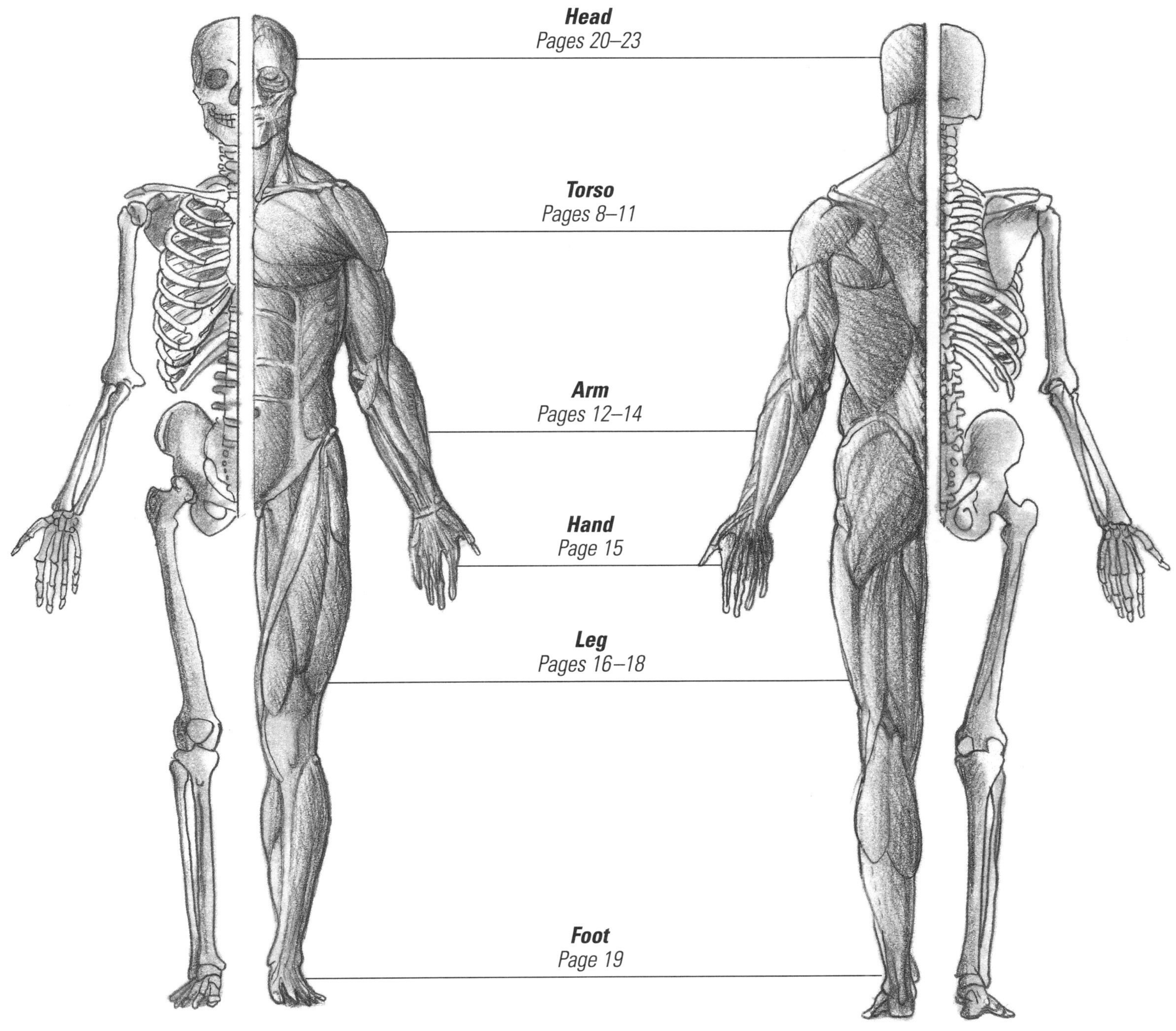

Visual Index This visual index includes many of the bones and muscles covered in this book. You can refer back to this page to test your newfound skills by identifying what you see here; if you need help, refer to the pages listed in the center of this chart.

EXPLORING THE TORSO: FRONT VIEW

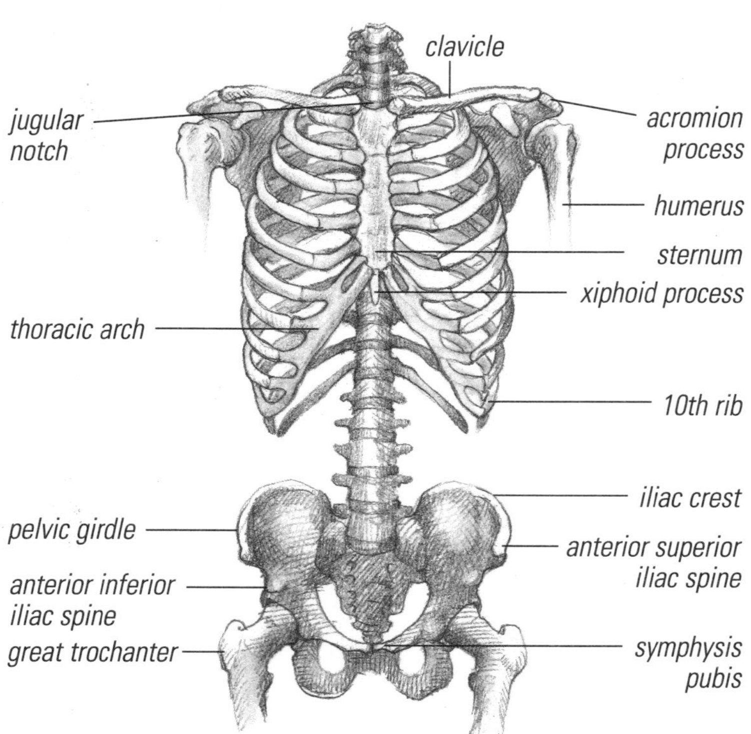

Skeleton Some parts of the skeletal system are important to the artist because they are prominent and so serve as visual landmarks. Several bones of the torso's frontal skeleton are obvious even beneath the skin, including the *clavicles, acromion processes, sternum, thoracic arch, 10th rib, anterior superior iliac spines,* and *great trochanters.* The spinal column comprises 24 vertebrae, divided into 3 sections: The *cervical* (or neck) region has 7 vertebrae, the *thoracic* (or chest) region has 12, and the *lumbar* (or lower back) region has 5.

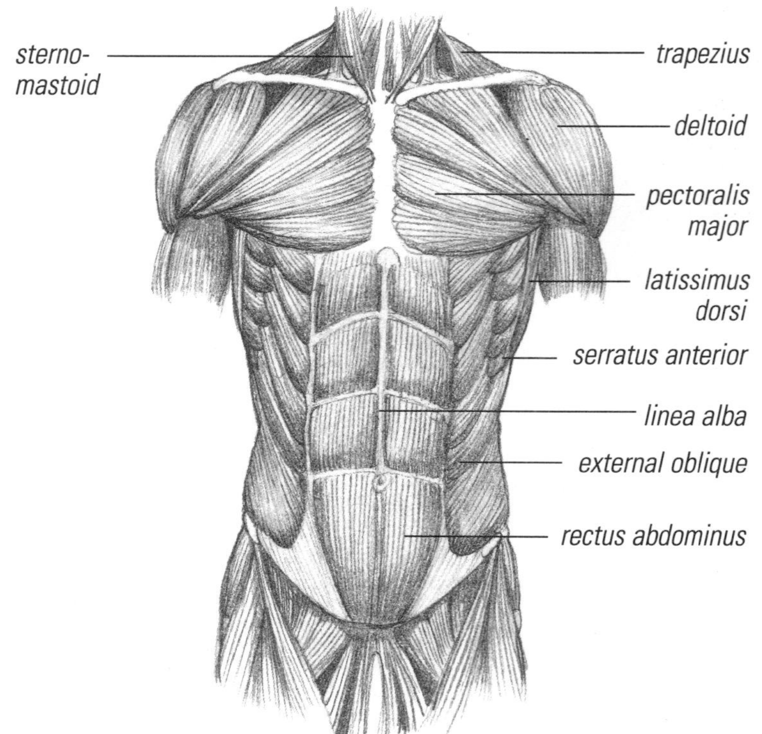

Trunk Muscles The torso's movement is dependent on and restricted by the spine—both the chest and the pelvis twist and turn on this fixed, yet flexible, column. And the relationship between the rib cage, the shoulders, and the pelvis creates the shape of the trunk muscles. The *pectoral* (breast) muscles are divided by the *sternum,* the *rectus abdominus* is divided by the *linea alba,* and the *external obliques*—which are interwoven with the *serratus anterior*—bind the eight lowest ribs to the *pelvic girdle.*

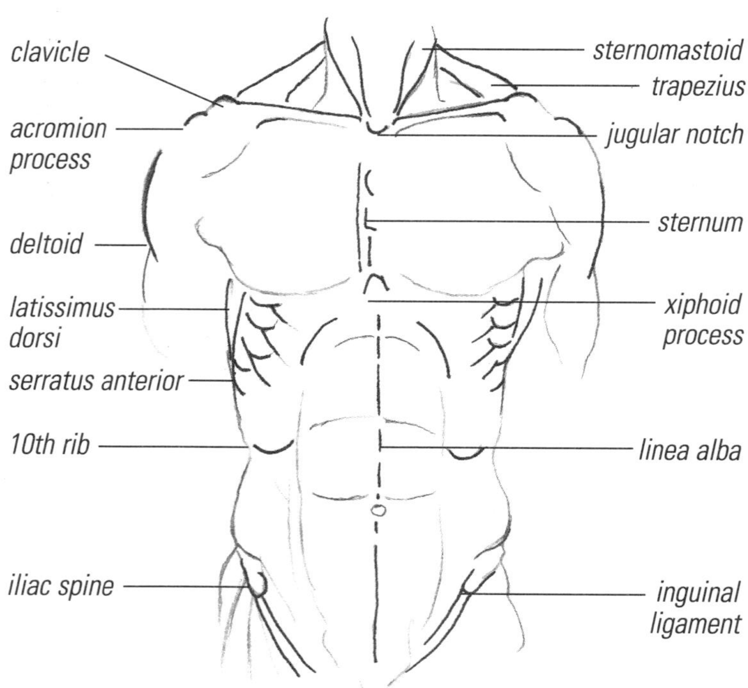

Diagram of Landmarks The observable muscles and bony landmarks labeled on the illustration above are the most important for artists who want to draw the torso's surface anatomy from the front view. Focus on accurately portraying these anatomical features to achieve a lifelike drawing, such as the example at right.

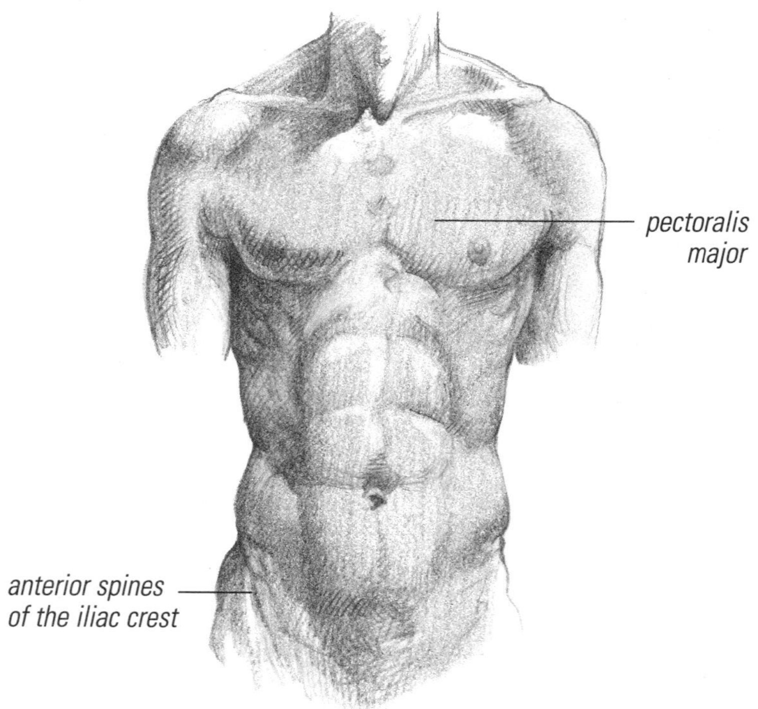

Drawing Tips Use the bony skeletal landmarks, which are apparent despite the layers of muscles, to guide the placement of the features. For example, the nipples align vertically with the *anterior spines* of the *iliac crest.* Note also that the *pectoralis major* sweeps across the chest and over to the arm, ending nearly horizontal to the nipples.

EXPLORING THE TORSO: BACK VIEW

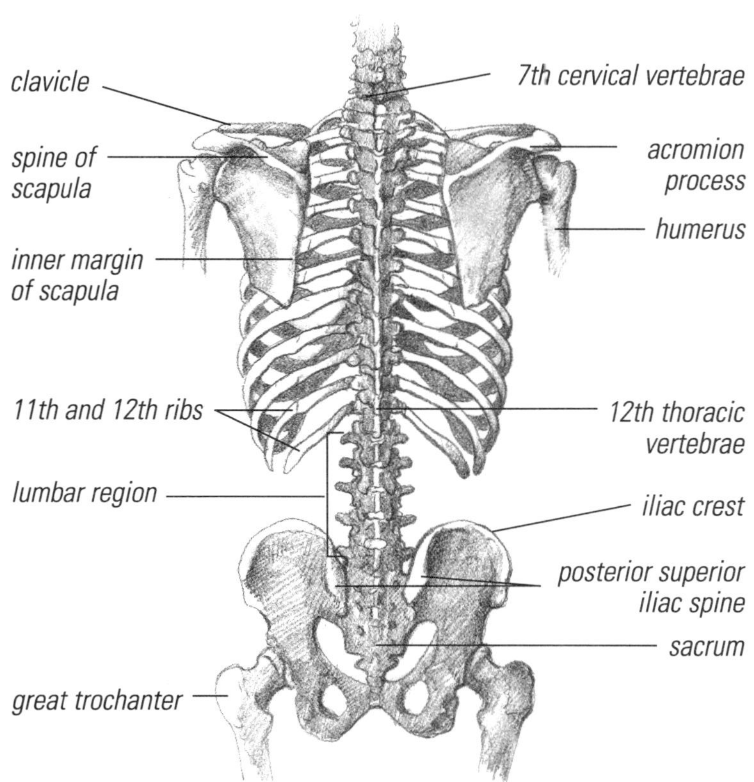

Skeleton The back is one of the most challenging parts of the body to draw because of its skeletal and muscular complexity. From the artist's point of view, the most important bones visible from the rear skeletal view are the *7th cervical vertebrae,* the *posterior superior iliac spines* (dimples on the pelvic girdle), and the *sacrum,* which together form *the sacral triangle*—a major anatomical landmark at the base of the spine.

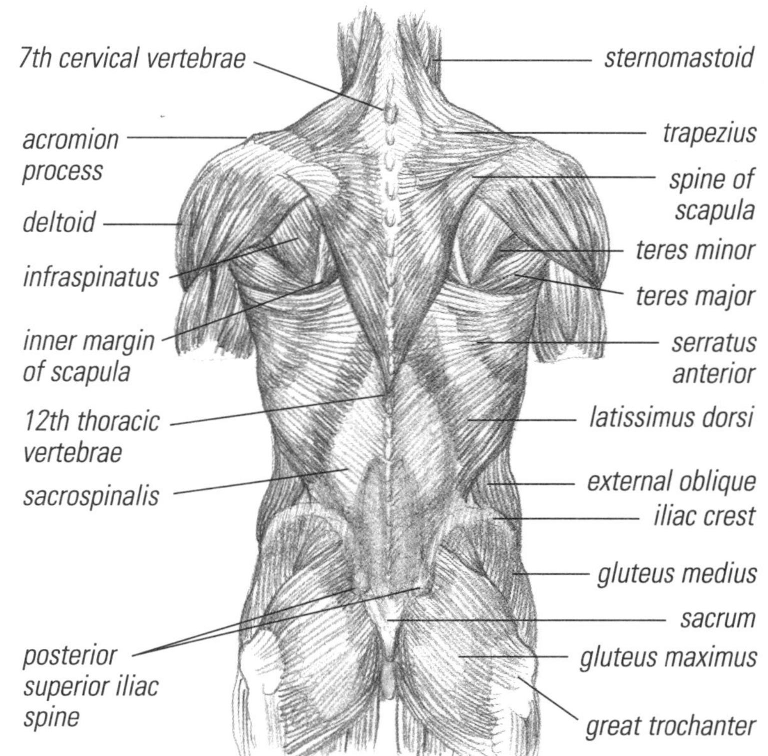

Trunk Muscles The back has many overlapping muscles; our focus will be on the upper layer, which is more immediately apparent to the eye. The *trapezius* connects the skull to the *scapula* (shoulder blade) muscles—*deltoid, infraspinatus, teres minor,* and *teres major*—which connect to the arm. The *latissimus dorsi* attaches under the arm, extending to the pelvis. And the *gluteus medius* bulges at the hip before meeting with the *gluteus maximus.*

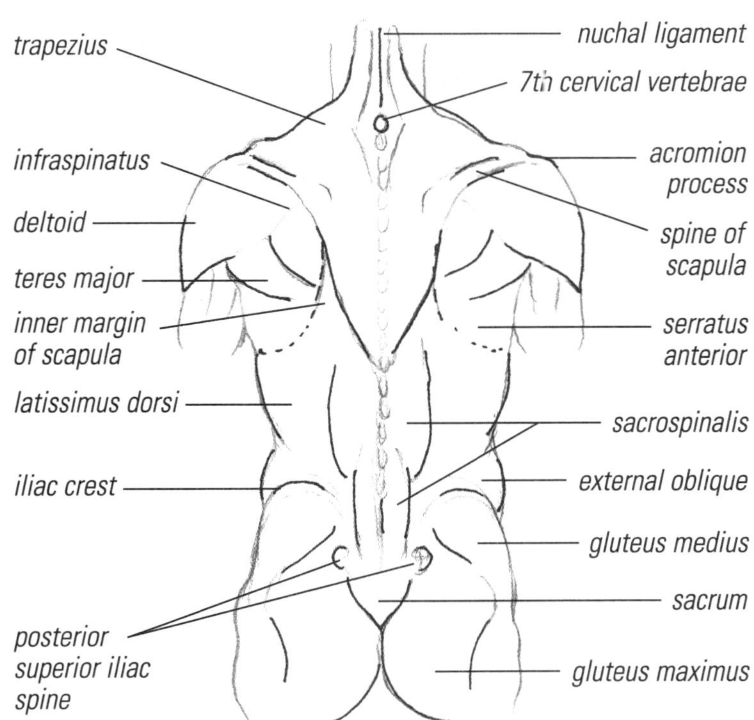

Diagram of Landmarks The observable muscles and bony landmarks labeled on the illustration above are the most important for artists who want to draw the torso's surface anatomy from the rear view. Focus on accurately rendering these anatomical markers to achieve a lifelike drawing, such as the example at right.

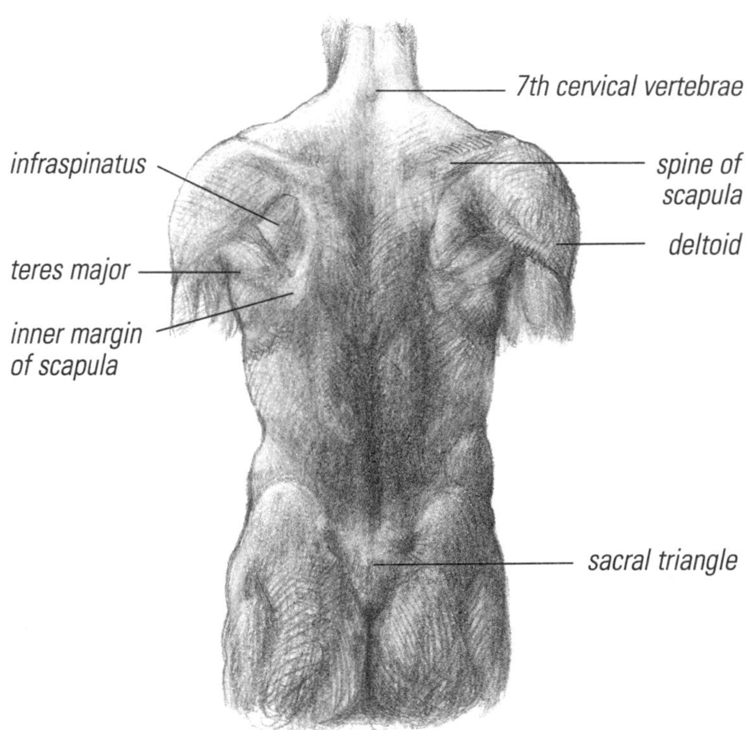

Drawing Tips Under the skin, back muscles are not easy to discern. However, the *trapezius, 7th cervical vertebrae, spine of scapula, inner margin of scapula, deltoid, infraspinatus,* and *terres major* are all fairly evident. To depict the *nuchal ligament, 7th cervical vertebrae, spinal column,* and *sacral triangle,* draw a long line and an upside-down triangle.

Exploring the Torso: Side View

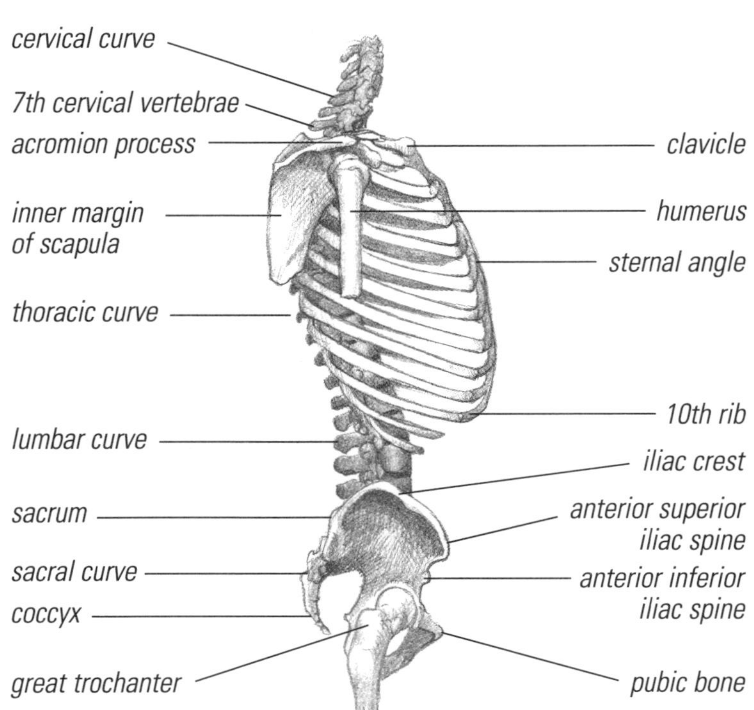

Skeleton The visual landmarks of the skeleton in profile are the *7th cervical vertebrae, acromion process, inner margin of scapula,* and backbone. The backbone's four curves—*cervical* (forward), *thoracic* (backward), *lumbar* (forward), and *sacral* (backward)—arrange the head, chest, and pelvic girdle over the legs for balance.

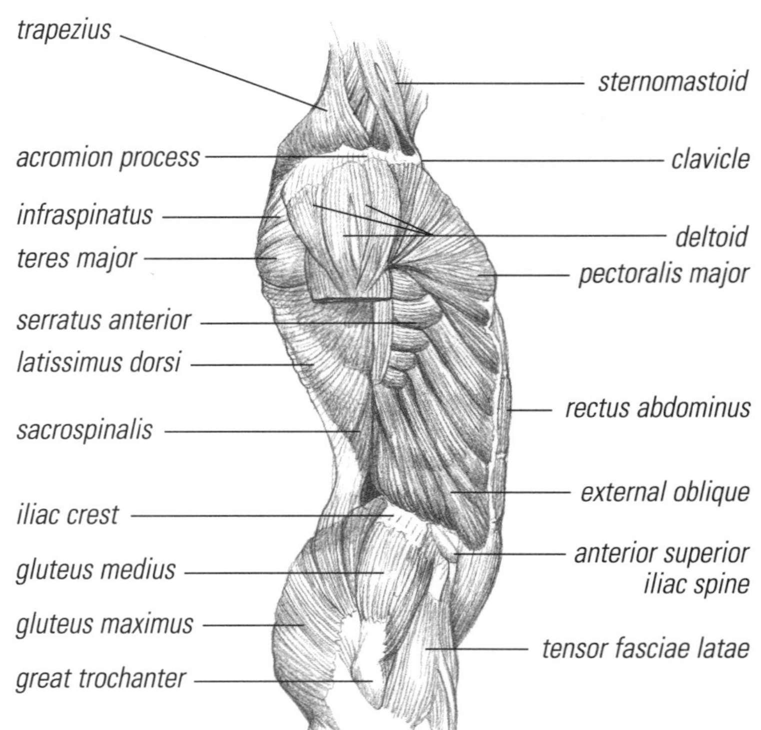

Trunk Muscles The upper torso muscles—as well as the *scapula,* which is anchored by muscle to the spine, ribs, and arms—follow and influence all arm movement. Mid-torso muscles, such as *external oblique, rectus abdominus,* and *latissimus dorsi,* bend, twist, and stabilize the rib cage and pelvis. Muscles below the *pelvic girdle* activate the legs.

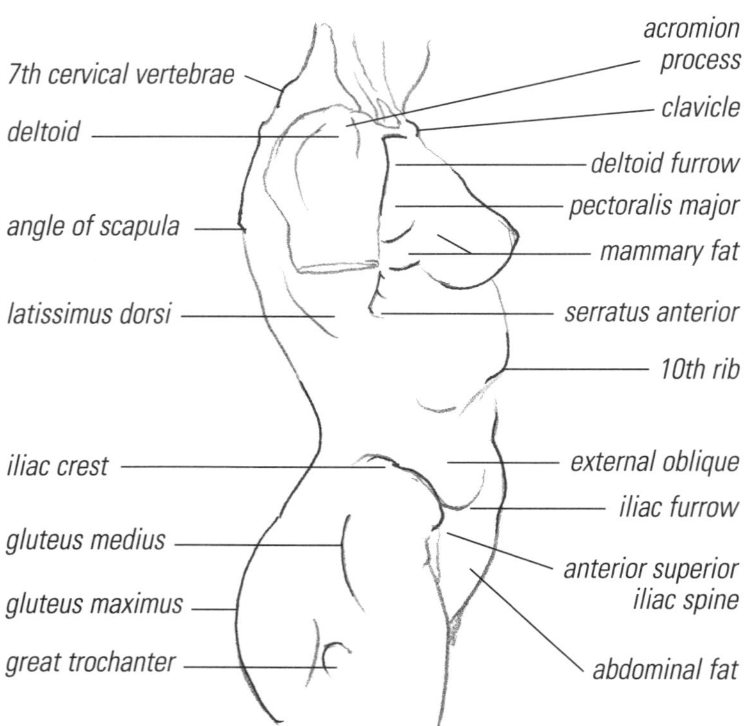

Diagram of Landmarks It is lack of fat in addition to degree of muscularity that determines surface definition. To render the female form, it's important to become familiar with fat deposit areas, including the flank *(iliac crest);* buttocks *(gluteus);* and stomach *(abdomin),* especially below the navel. *Mammary* fat accounts for the smoothness of the breast.

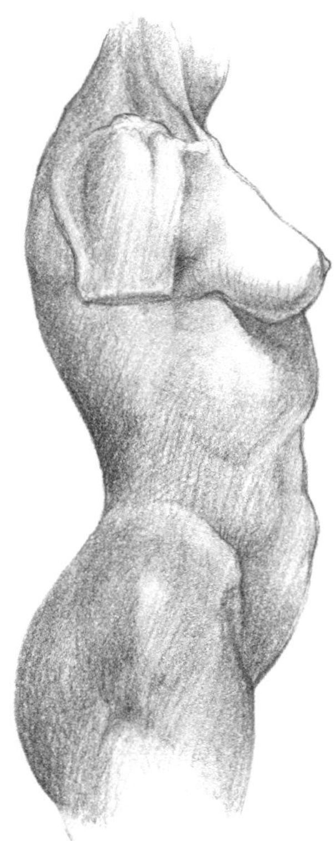

Drawing Tips Female figures display a more fluid contour than do male figures, largely because of the female's extra fatty layer, which serves a reproductive purpose but also obscures muscular form. Muscular structure is basically the same for both sexes, but the width and angle of the pelvis makes the skeleton more recognizably male or female.

EXPLORING THE TORSO: TIPS

FRONT VIEW

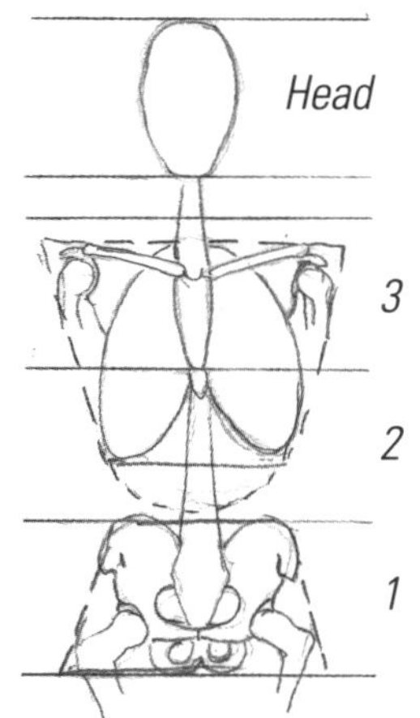

Proportion The *pelvic girdle* is about 1 head high, and the torso—from *trochanters* to *7th cervicle vertebrae*—is about 3 heads high.

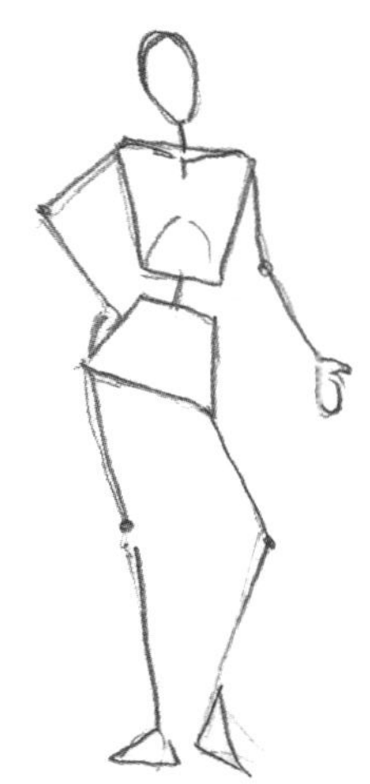

Simplified Figurette Sketching with simple lines and basic shapes is a good way to establish the base of a figure drawing.

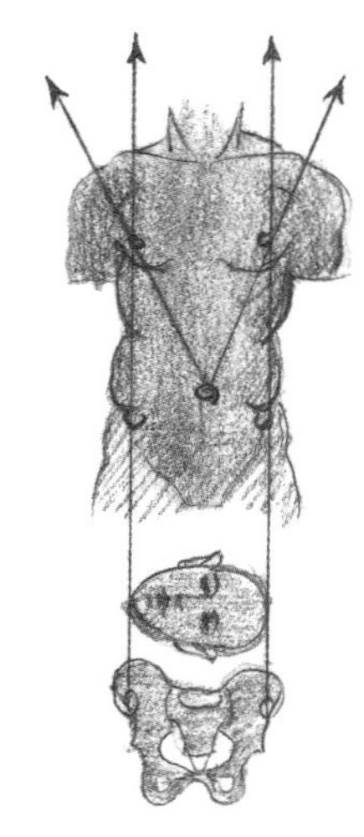

Tips The nipples, 1 head-width apart, are vertically aligned with pelvic landmarks and diagonally aligned with the *acromion processes.*

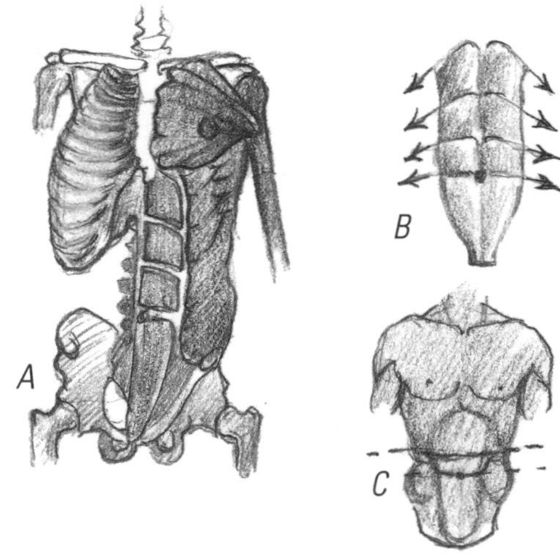

Detail Note the relationship between the skeletal and muscular structures (A). The *linea alba* (interrupting tendons) of the *rectus abdominis* create a "six pack" appearance as they arch progressively higher toward the *sternum* (B). Two of the interrupting tendons line up with the *10th rib* and the navel (C).

BACK VIEW

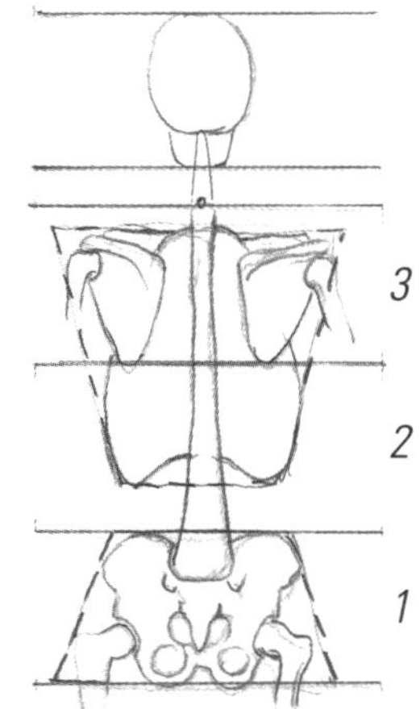

Trapezoids represent the overall bone structure of the torso from both front and rear views. Here you can see the same three-part division.

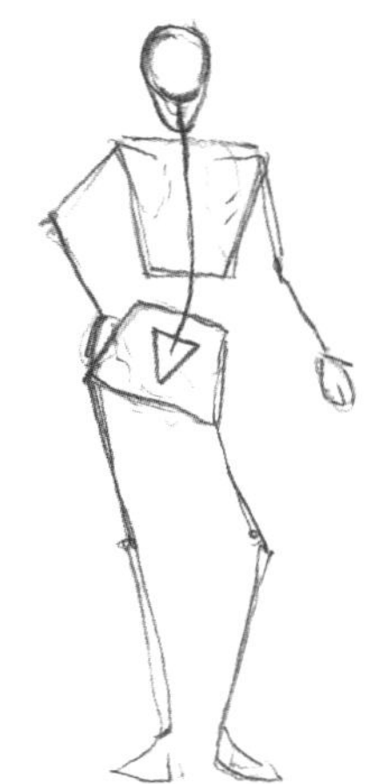

This simplified sketch from the back view includes an important feature: a line from the *7th cervicle vertebrae* to the *sacral triangle.*

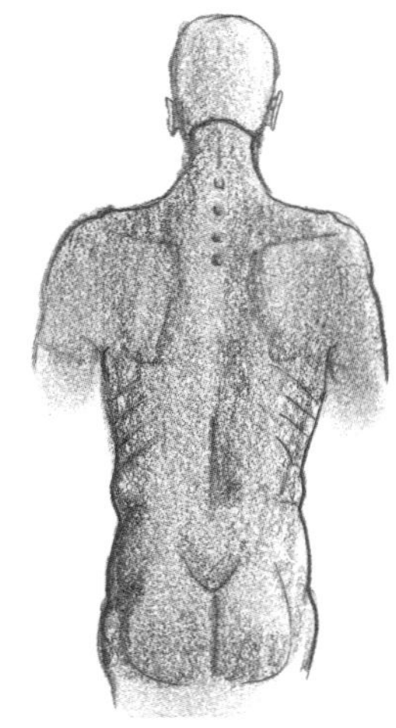

On an erect figure, the bones of both the lower ribs and the upper spine are apparent, while the *lumbar* region looks like a furrow.

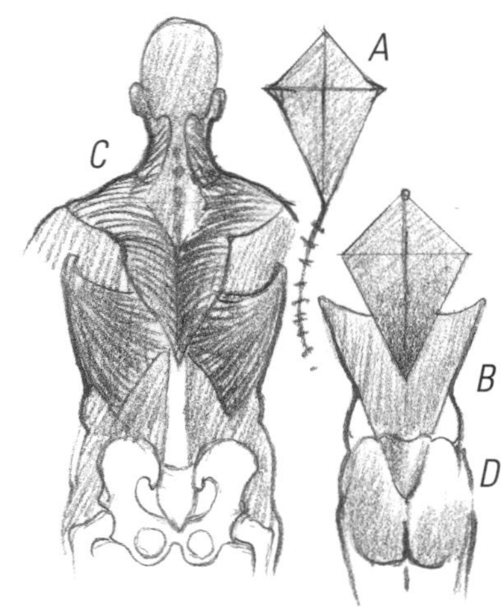

The shape of the *trapezius* is similar to that of a kite (A) or a four-pointed star (C). The simplified shape of the *latissimus dorsi* suggests the appearance of an upside-down triangle (B), with a diamond-shaped sheath removed from its upside-down apex (D).

SIDE VIEW

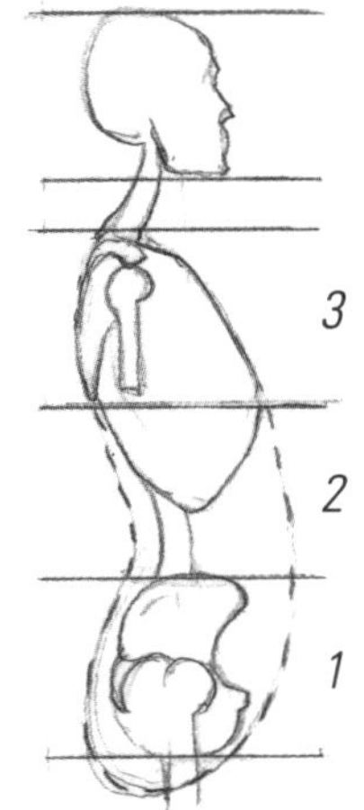

The simplified torso from the side view has a bean-shaped appearance, but the same proportional divisions of the torso apply.

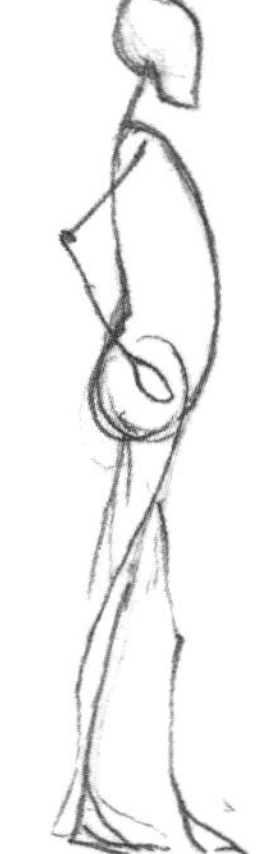

The simplified figurette in profile makes use of the bean and oval shapes that appear in the proportional drawing at left.

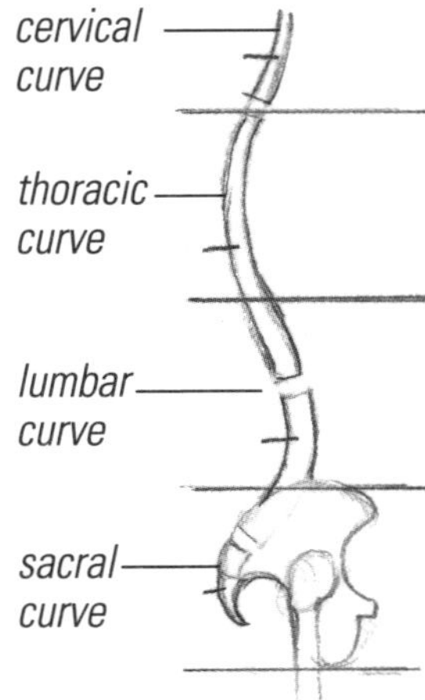

Each spinal segment curves more as the column descends toward the *sacrum.* The *thoracic* region has the longest curve.

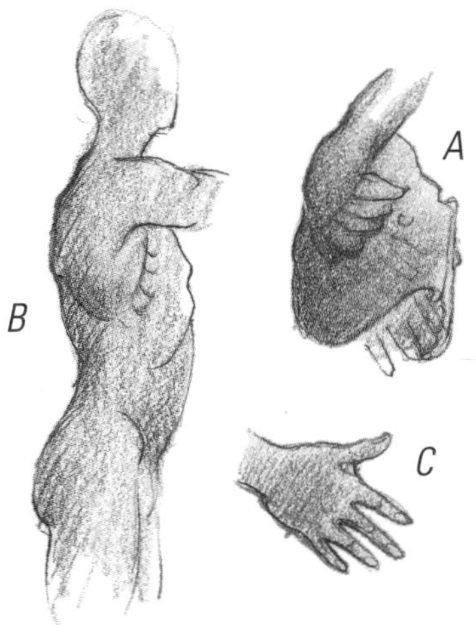

The *serratus anterior* muscle starts alongside the first eight ribs, then ends at the inner margin of the *scapula* (A). Its main mass appears as a bulge underneath the *latissimus dorsi* (B). At the muscle's origin (on the ribs), it looks a little like the fingers of a hand (C).

DEPICTING THE ARM: FRONT VIEW

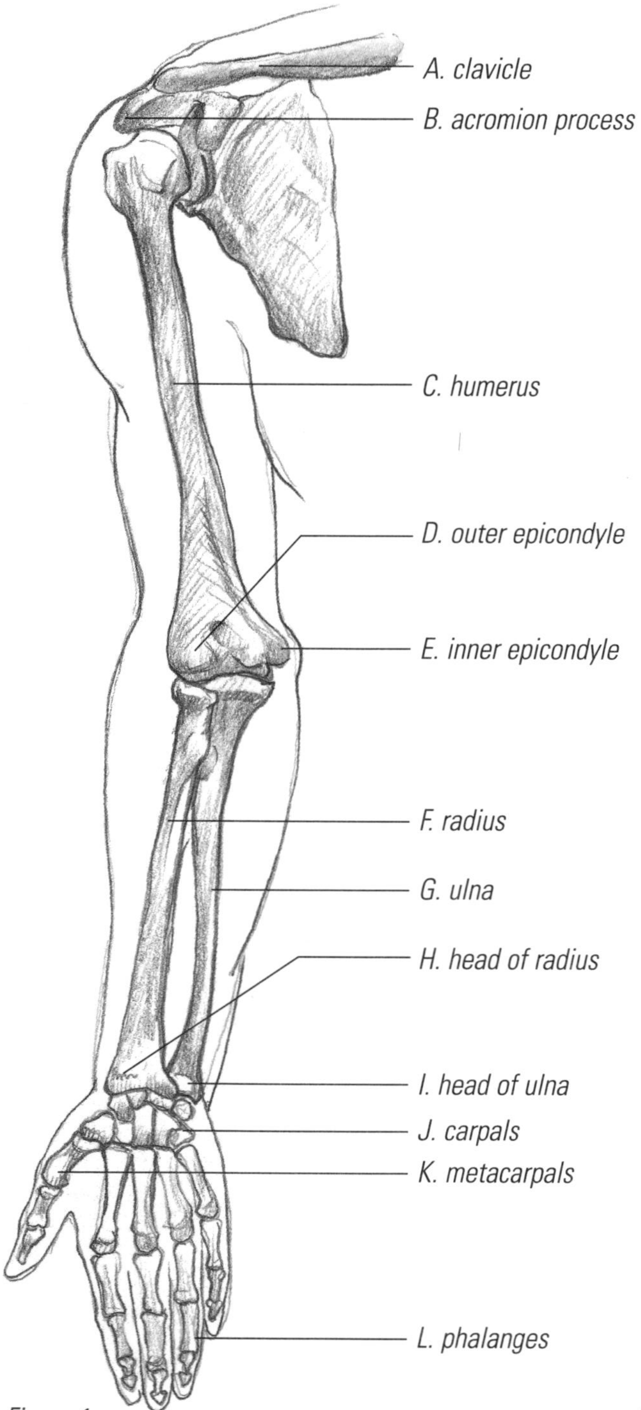

Figure 1

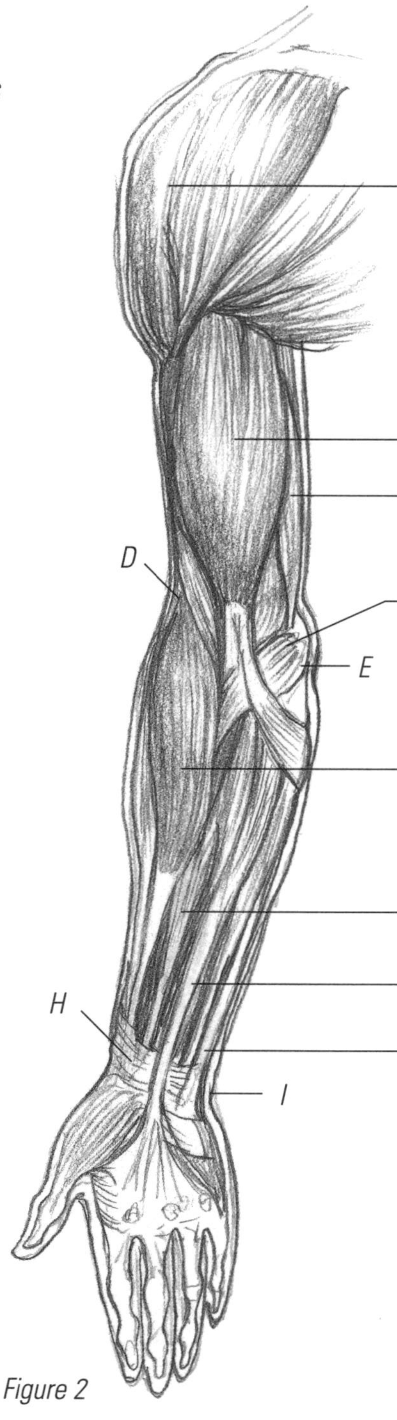

Figure 2

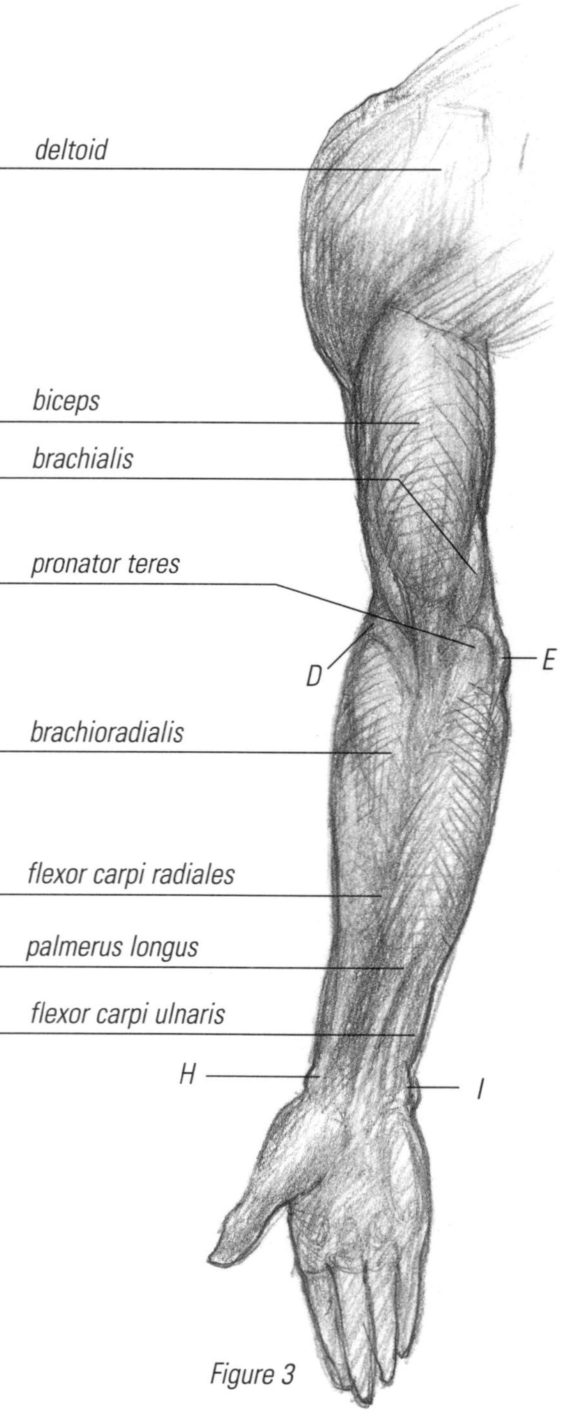

Figure 3

Bones The underlying skeletal structure determines much of the overall shape of the arm (figure 1). Several elements of this substructure, such as the *inner epicondyle* (E), act as visual landmarks that are identifiable even under layers of muscle (figure 2) and skin (figure 3).

Muscles The upper and lower portions of the arm each consist of three major muscle masses. The *bicep* and *brachialis* of the upper arm bend the lower arm, the *tricep* (see page 13) straightens it, and the *deltoid* raises the entire arm. In the lower arm, the flexors *(flexor carpi radiales, palmerus longus, and flexor carpi ulnaris)* bend the palm and clench the fingers; the extensors on the back of the arm (see page 13) straighten the palm and open the fingers; and the supinators *(brachioradialis,* see page 13), attached to the *outer epicondyle* (D, figure 1) on the outside arm, rotate the hand outward. A fourth, smaller muscle, the *pronator teres,* rotates the palm inward.

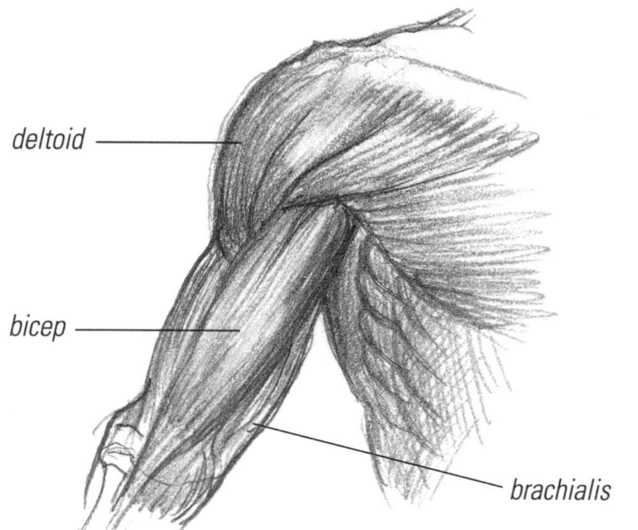

Drawing Tips The *bicep* does not extend across the full width of the upper arm. The *deltoid* inserts in between the *brachialis* and the *bicep.*

DEPICTING THE ARM: BACK VIEW

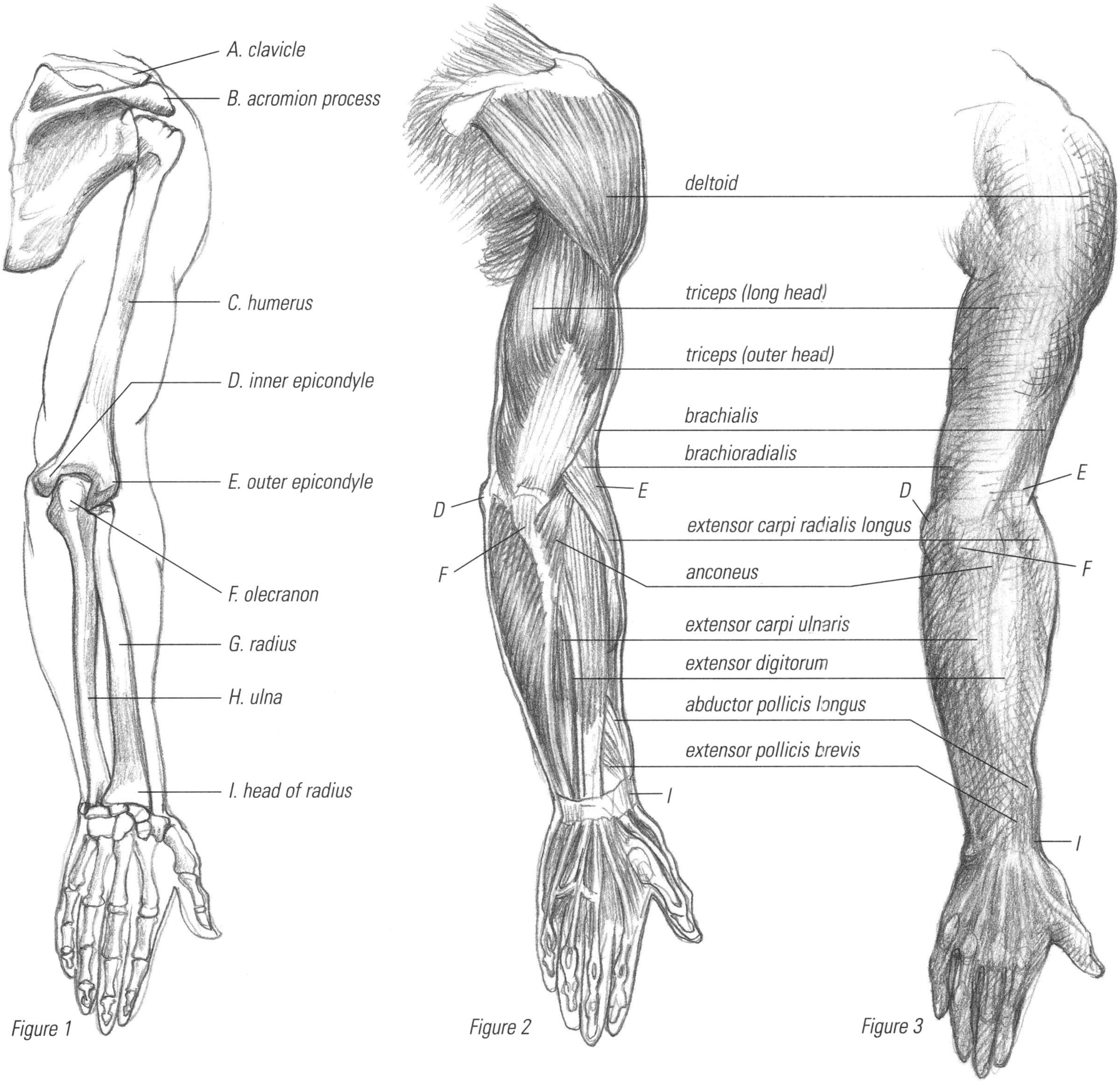

Figure 1

Figure 2

Figure 3

Bones Much of the overall shape of the arm in the back view is determined by the underlying skeletal structure, just as with the front view. The *inner* and *outer epicondyle* (D and E), are again identifiable, even under layers of muscle. And from this view, the *olecranon,* or elbow (F), is also evident.

Muscles Muscles work in opposing pairs: *Flexors* (see page 12, figures 2 and 3) pull and *extensors* extend, moving in the opposite direction. When a flexor or extensor muscle becomes active, its opposite becomes passive. From the back view, when the hand is pronate (illustrated in figures 2 and 3 above), extensor groups are the most prominent muscles. On the upper arm, the *tricep* is the most visible extensor. On the lower arm, *extensor carpi radialis longus, extensor carpi ulnaris,* and *extensor digitorum*, which all originate on the *outer epicondyle,* are evident.

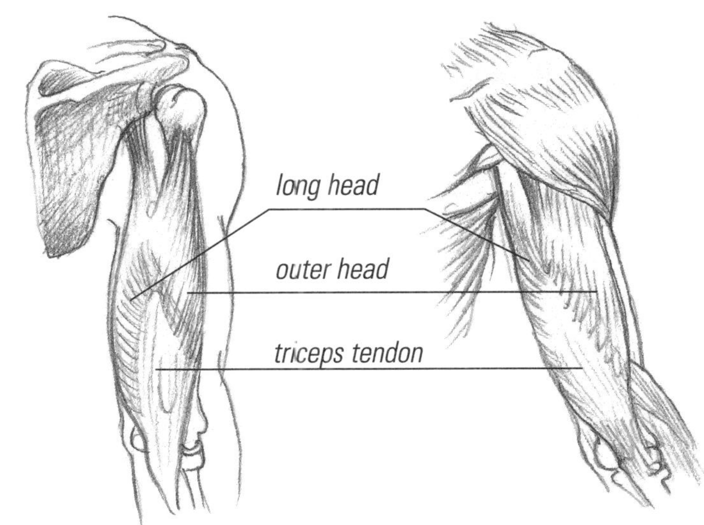

Drawing Tips The *tricep* has three heads (the long and outer heads are shown here; the medial head lies beneath). All share a common tendon: a flattened form on the back of the upper arm.

DEPICTING THE ARM: SIDE VIEW

CLENCHED FIST

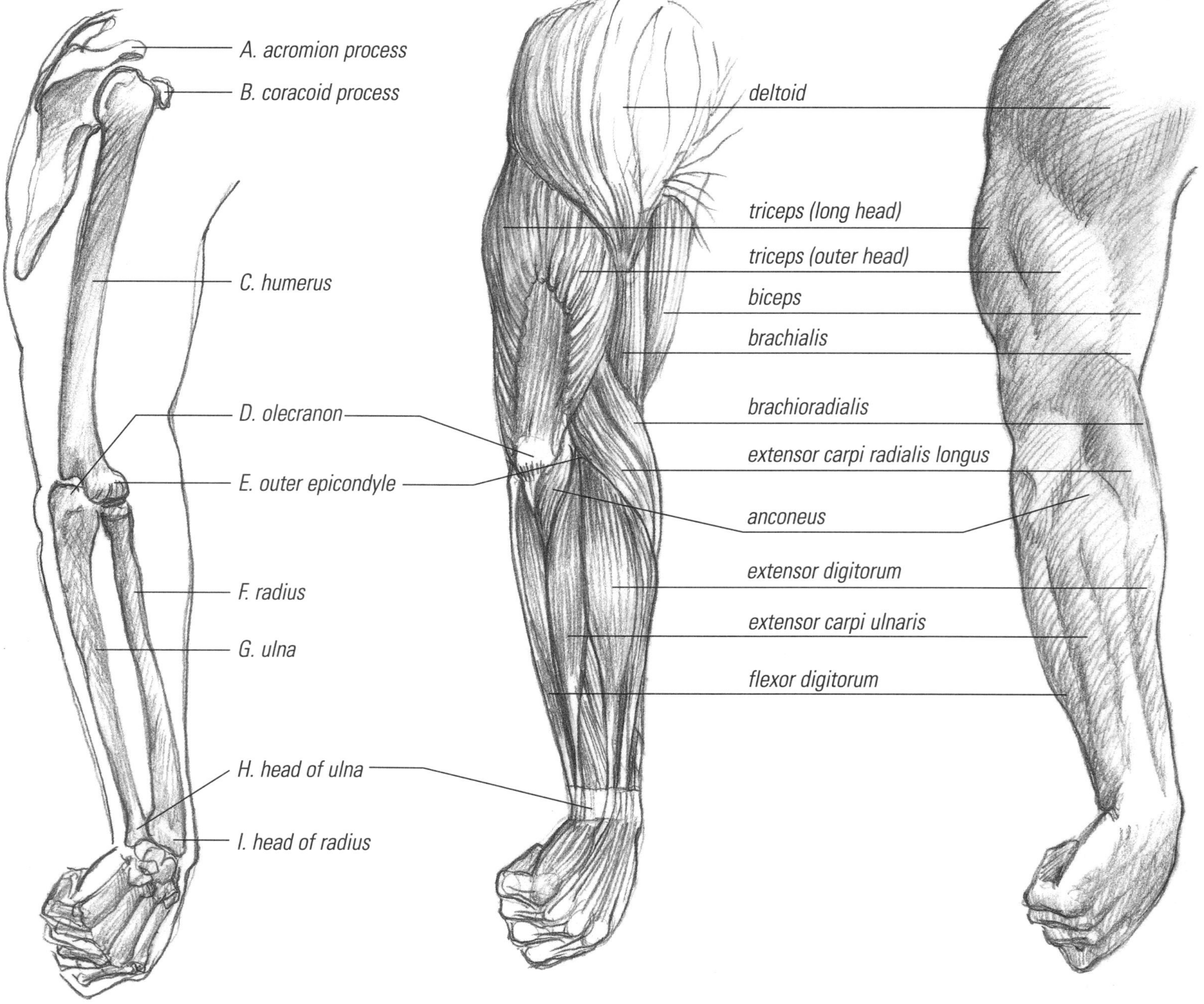

A. acromion process
B. coracoid process
C. humerus
D. olecranon
E. outer epicondyle
F. radius
G. ulna
H. head of ulna
I. head of radius

deltoid
triceps (long head)
triceps (outer head)
biceps
brachialis
brachioradialis
extensor carpi radialis longus
anconeus
extensor digitorum
extensor carpi ulnaris
flexor digitorum

Bones Here the arm is not viewed in full profile; rather it is seen from an angle that is a combination of a side view and a back view. Because of the angle, the bony landmarks most apparent under the muscle are the *olecranon, outer epicondyle,* and *head of ulna.*

Muscles The side view provides a good angle for observing the extensors and flexors of the upper and lower arm. The *brachio-radialis,* located where the upper and lower arms meet, is particularly important. It originates on the lateral side of the *humerus* (C), above the *outer epicondyle* (E), and then attaches to the lateral side of the wrist above the *head of radius* (I).

Drawing Tips

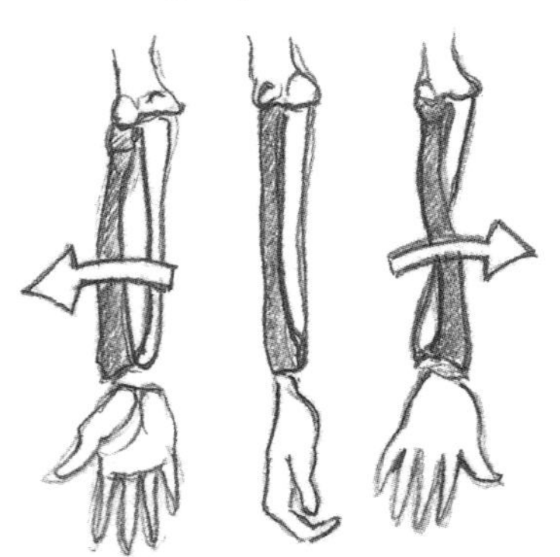

Bent Arm

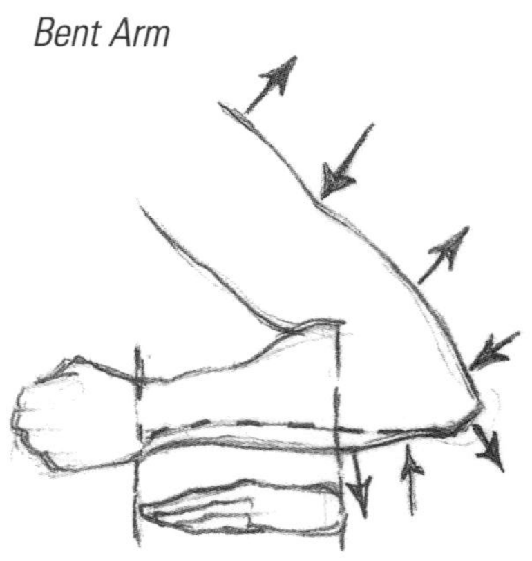

Rotated Arm

The *brachioradialis* is responsible for turning the palm up *(supinate),* and the *pronator teres* (see page 12) for turning the palm down *(pronate).* The *radius* (shaded) rotates around the fixed *ulna,* permitting pronation and supination of the palm.

The span between the inside bend of the elbow and the wrist is usually about one hand length. The arrows show the inward and outward curvature of the muscles, and the dashed line shows the line of the *ulna,* called the "ulnar furrow."

PORTRAYING THE HAND

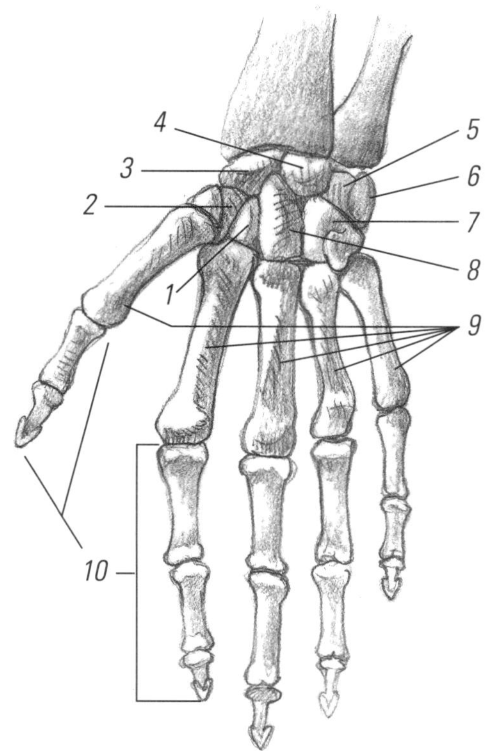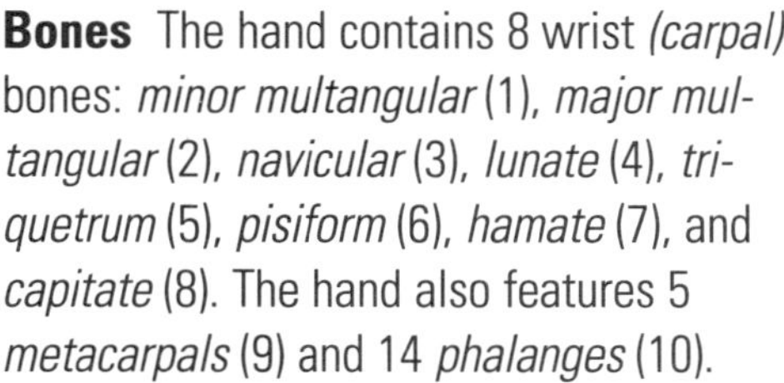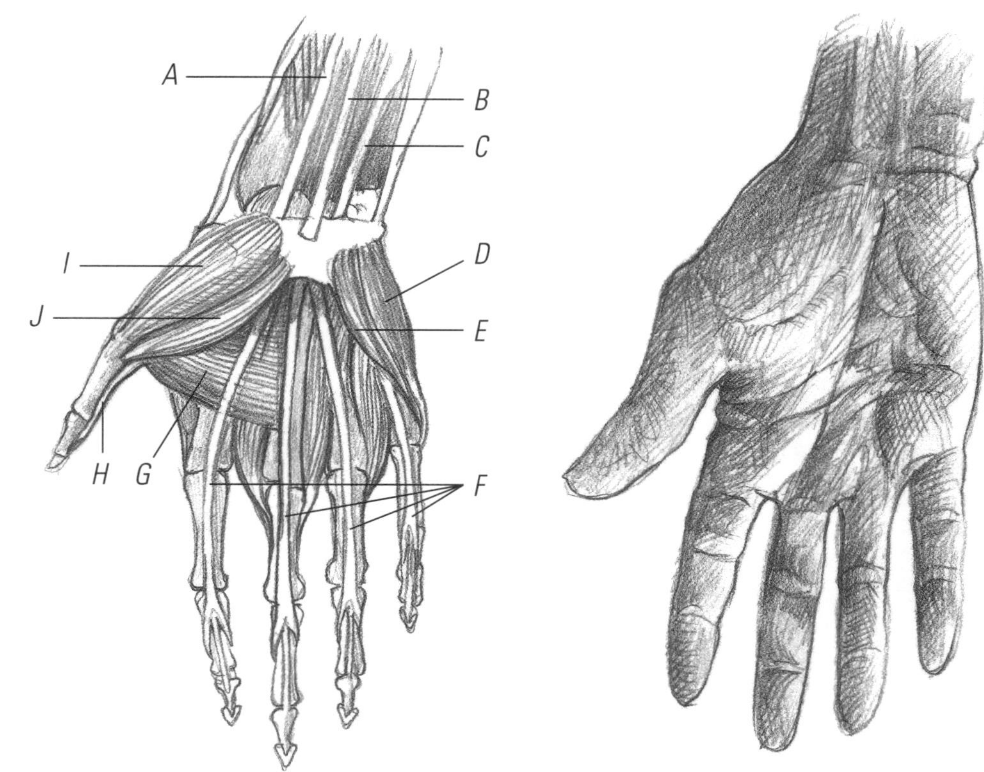

Bones The hand contains 8 wrist *(carpal)* bones: *minor multangular* (1), *major multangular* (2), *navicular* (3), *lunate* (4), *triquetrum* (5), *pisiform* (6), *hamate* (7), and *capitate* (8). The hand also features 5 *metacarpals* (9) and 14 *phalanges* (10).

Muscles The *flexor tendons* (A, B, C) from the forearm muscles (see page 12) extend into the hand. The teardrop-shaped muscle masses, the *thenar eminence abductors* of the thumb (I, J) and the *hypothenar eminence abductor* (D) and *flexor* (E) of the little finger, are known as the "palmer hand muscles." The *adductor* of the thumb (G) lies under the *flexor tendons* (F). The visible creases of the palm result from the way the skin folds over the fat and muscles of the hand.

BACK

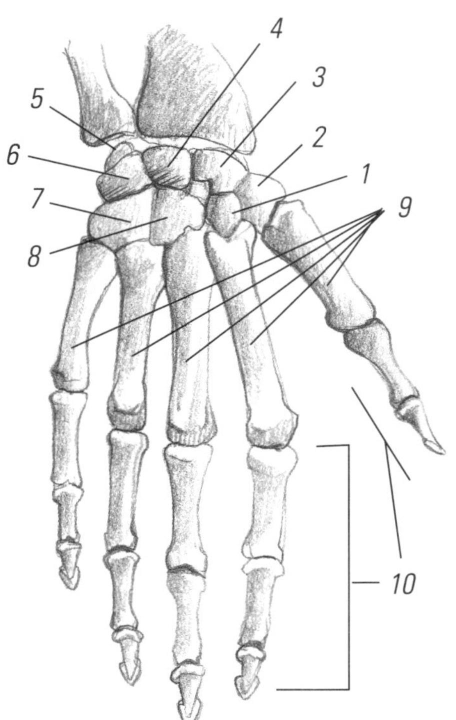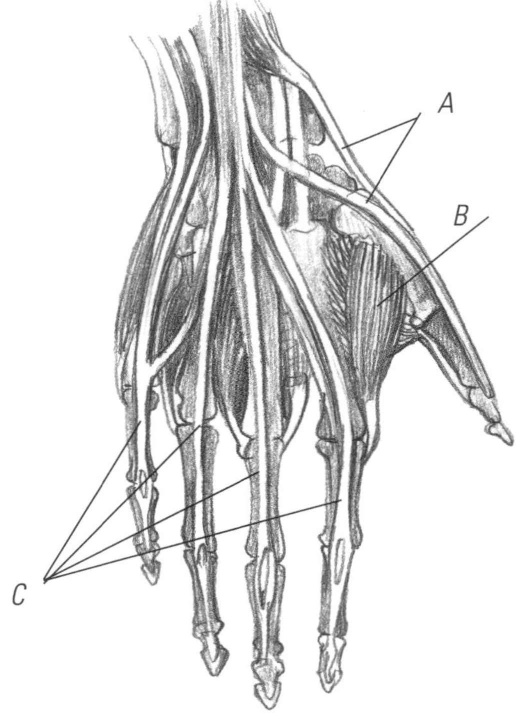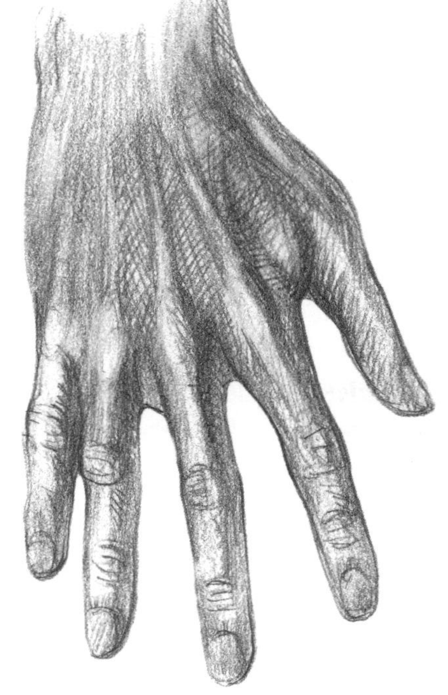

Bones From this view of the hand, all the same bones are visible, but the carpal bones appear convex rather than concave. From this angle, the bones have more influence on the shape of the fleshed-out hand.

Muscles Whereas the palm side of the hand is muscular and fatty, the back of the hand is bony and full of tendons. The *extensor tendons* of the thumb (A) are visible when contracted, as are the other four *extensor tendons* (C). The *first dorsal interosseous* (B) is the largest of the four *dorsal interosseous* muscles, and it is the only one that shows its form through the skin's surface; when the thumb is flexed, this muscle appears as a bulging teardrop shape.

Sketching the Leg: Front View

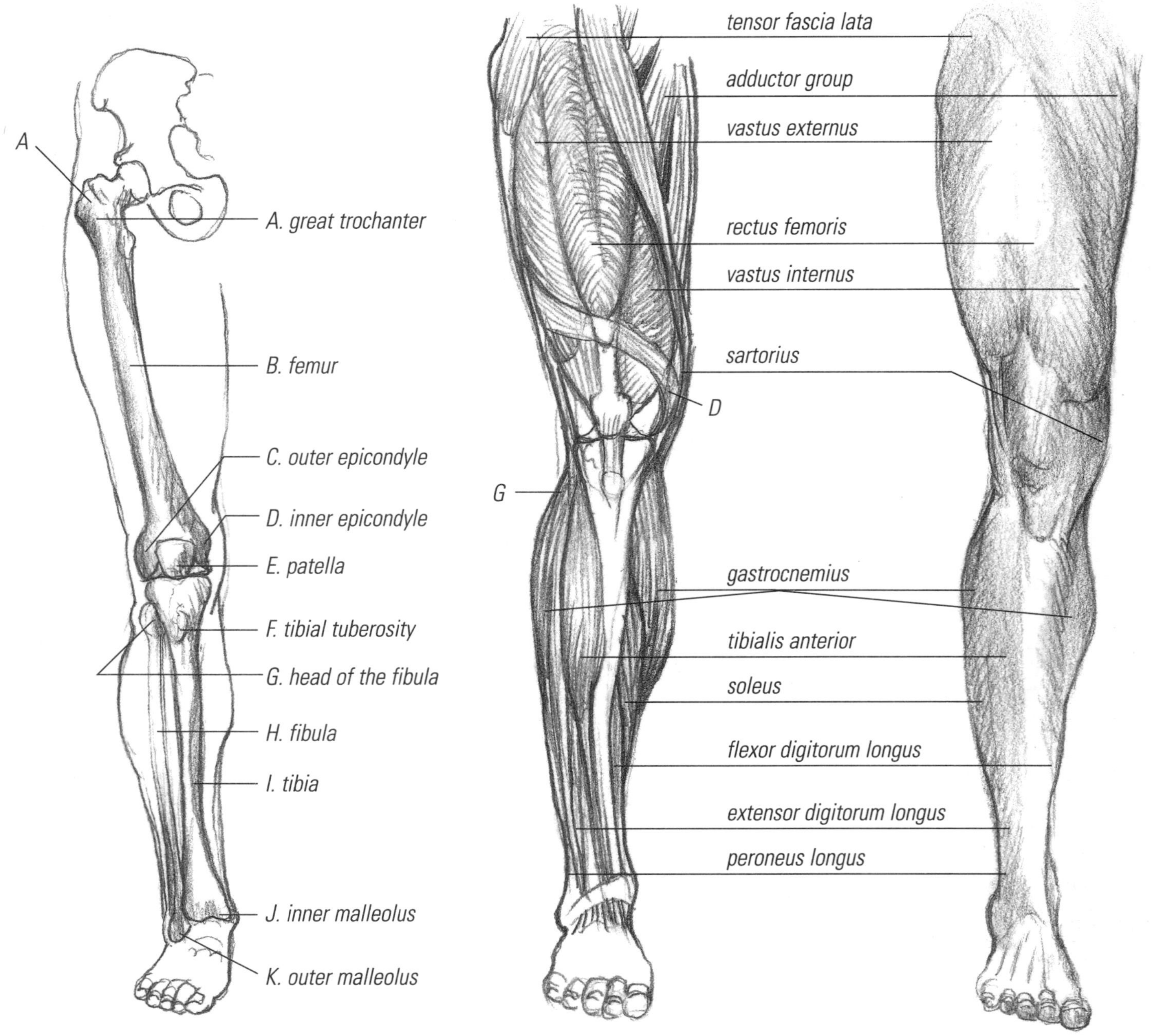

A. great trochanter

B. femur

C. outer epicondyle

D. inner epicondyle

E. patella

F. tibial tuberosity

G. head of the fibula

H. fibula

I. tibia

J. inner malleolus

K. outer malleolus

tensor fascia lata

adductor group

vastus externus

rectus femoris

vastus internus

sartorius

gastrocnemius

tibialis anterior

soleus

flexor digitorum longus

extensor digitorum longus

peroneus longus

Bones The *femur* (B), with its *great trochanter* at the top (A) and *outer epicondyles* (C) and *inner epicondyles* (D) at the base, is the heaviest and longest bone of the skeletal system. The knee cap (*patella*) sits in between the *outer epicondyles* and *inner epicondyles* on the patellar surface. The lower leg consists of the thick *tibia* (I) and the slender *fibula* (H). The *tibial tuberosity* (F) and *head of the fibula* (G) are important landmarks at the top, as are the ankle bones (the *inner malleolus* and *outer malleolus*).

Muscles The upper leg has four major muscle masses: *vastus externus,* which attaches to the knee cap (E); *rectus femoris,* which engulfs the *patella* (E) and continues toward the *tibial tuberosity* (F); *vastus internus,* a medial bulge; and the *adductor group* on the inside of the leg. There are also two other masses: the *tensor fascia lata* and the *sartorius.* The *sartorius* is the longest muscle in the body. The lower leg has six long muscles visible: *gastrocnemius,* protruding on both sides; *tibialis anterior,* running along the shin toward the big toe; *soleus; flexor digitorum longus; extensor digitorum longus;* and *peroneus longus.*

Drawing Tips The legs angle in toward the middle, positioning the body's weight over the gravitational center. (See figures 1 and 2.) The muscle masses on the outside of the leg are higher than those on the inside. (See figure 3.) The ankles are just the reverse—high inside, low outside.

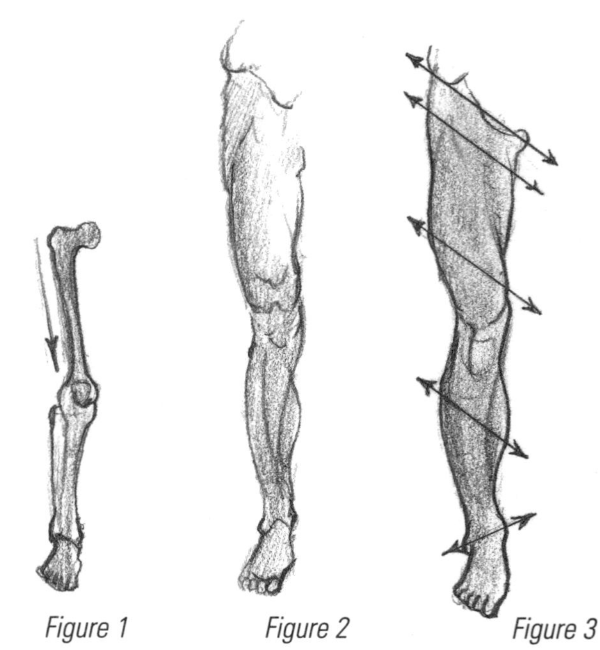

Figure 1　　　　Figure 2　　　　Figure 3

Sketching the Leg: Back View

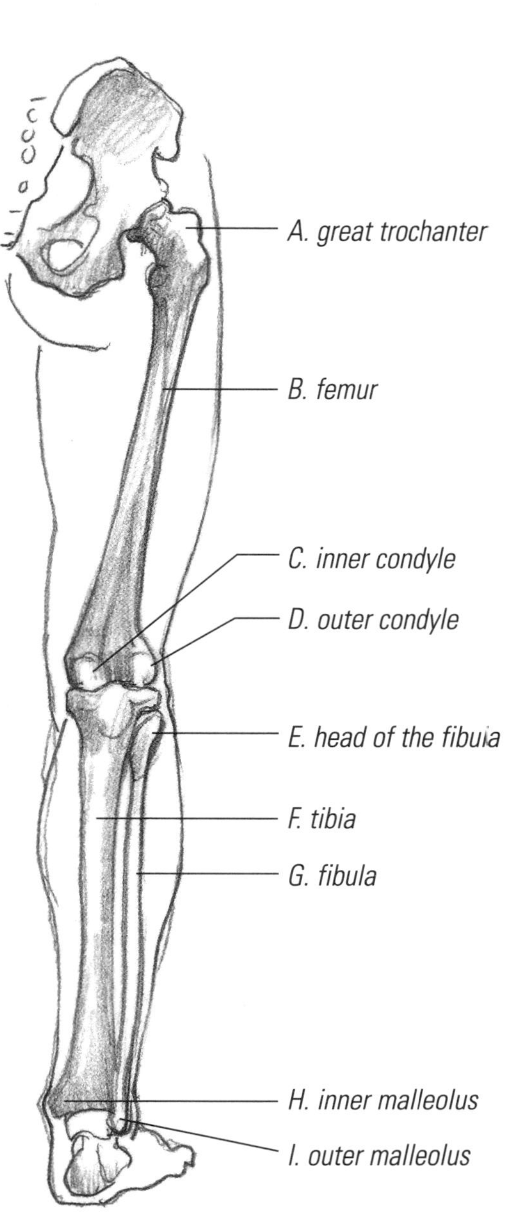

- A. great trochanter
- B. femur
- C. inner condyle
- D. outer condyle
- E. head of the fibula
- F. tibia
- G. fibula
- H. inner malleolus
- I. outer malleolus

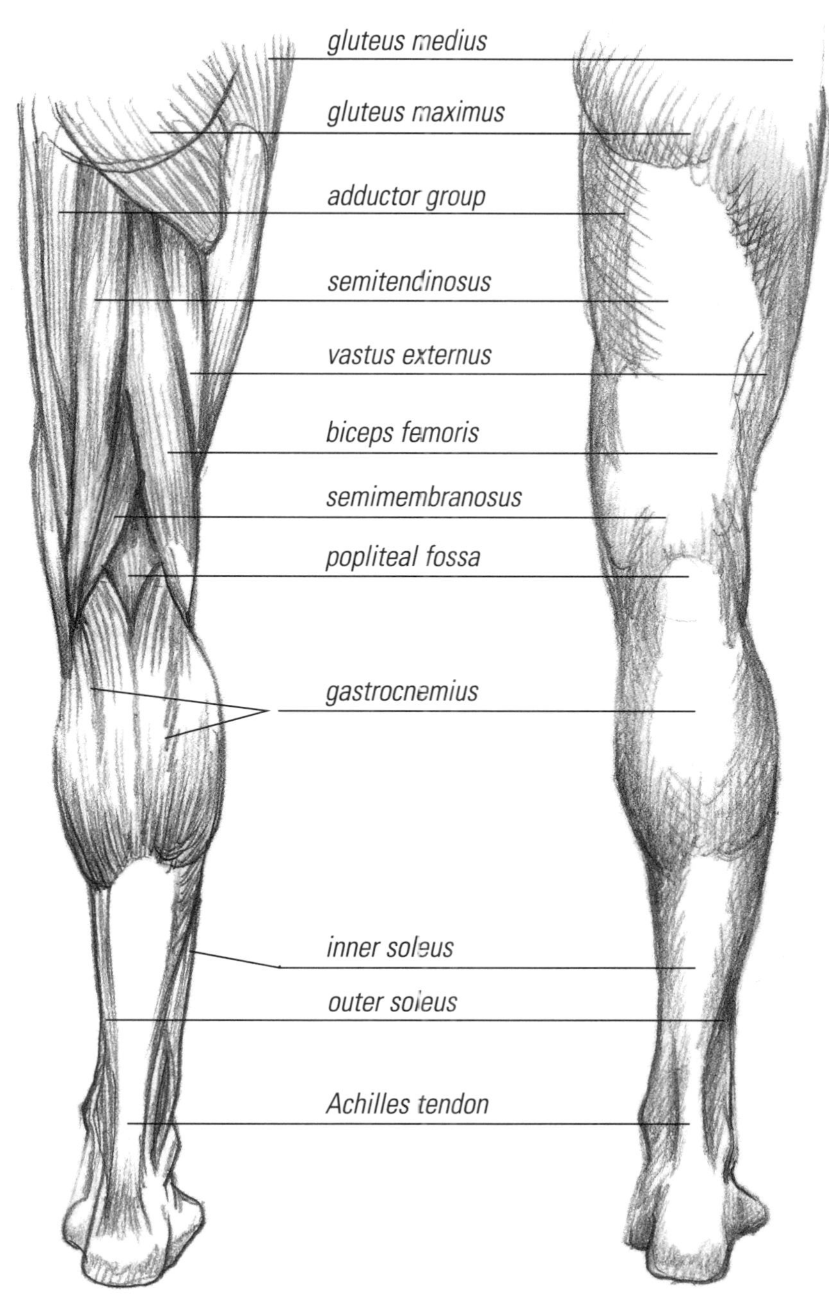

Bones From the back view, the same leg bones that appear in the front view are visible. Their appearance is slightly altered, however, because the bone attachments in the front are designed to allow muscles to extend, and the back attachment is designed for muscles to flex.

Muscles The upper leg consists of five large muscle masses: *gluteus maximus; gluteus medius;* the hamstring group (*biceps femoris, semitendinosus,* and *semimembranosus*); the *adductor group;* and the *vastus externus,* which can be seen peeking out from behind the *biceps femoris.*

The lower leg also features five masses: three larger ones and two smaller. The larger masses are the two heads of the calf: the *gastrocnemius* and the *Achilles tendon,* which connects to the heel bone. The two smaller masses are the *inner soleus* and *outer soleus.* Also notice the hollow area behind the knee where the calf tendons attach, called the "popliteal fossa"; this fatty hollow makes deep knee bends possible.

Drawing Tips The calf is lower and rounder on the inside than it is on the outside. (See figure 1.)

The hamstring tendons grip below the knee on both sides, almost like a pair of tongs. (See figure 2.)

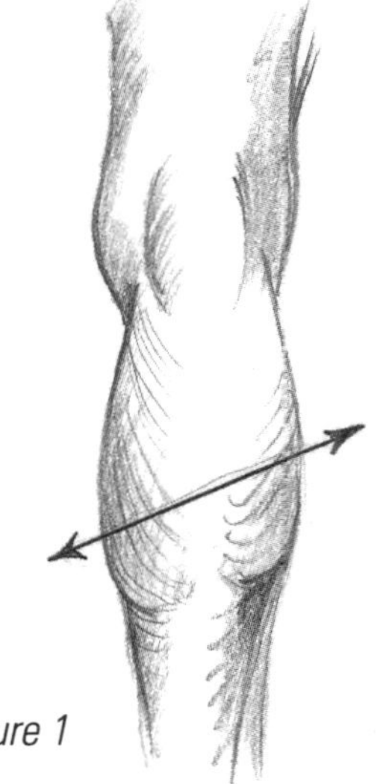

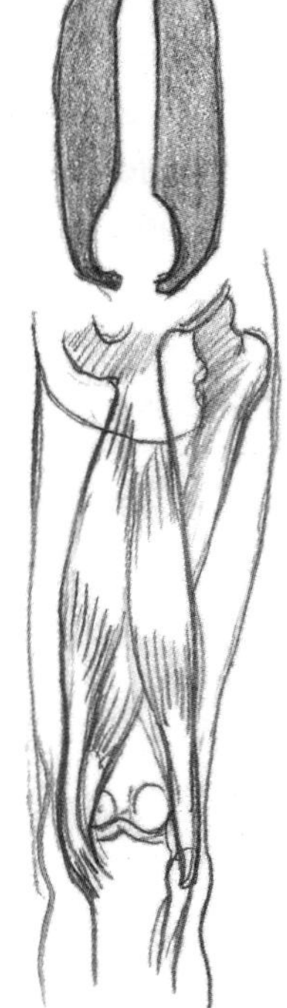

Figure 1

Figure 2

Sketching the Leg: Side View

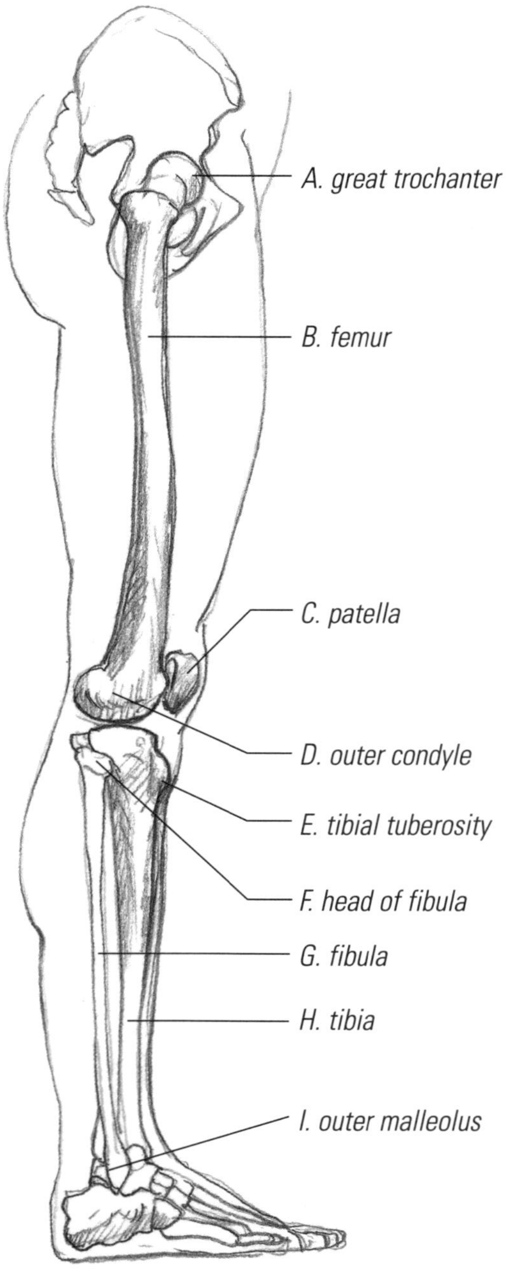

A. great trochanter

B. femur

C. patella

D. outer condyle

E. tibial tuberosity

F. head of fibula

G. fibula

H. tibia

I. outer malleolus

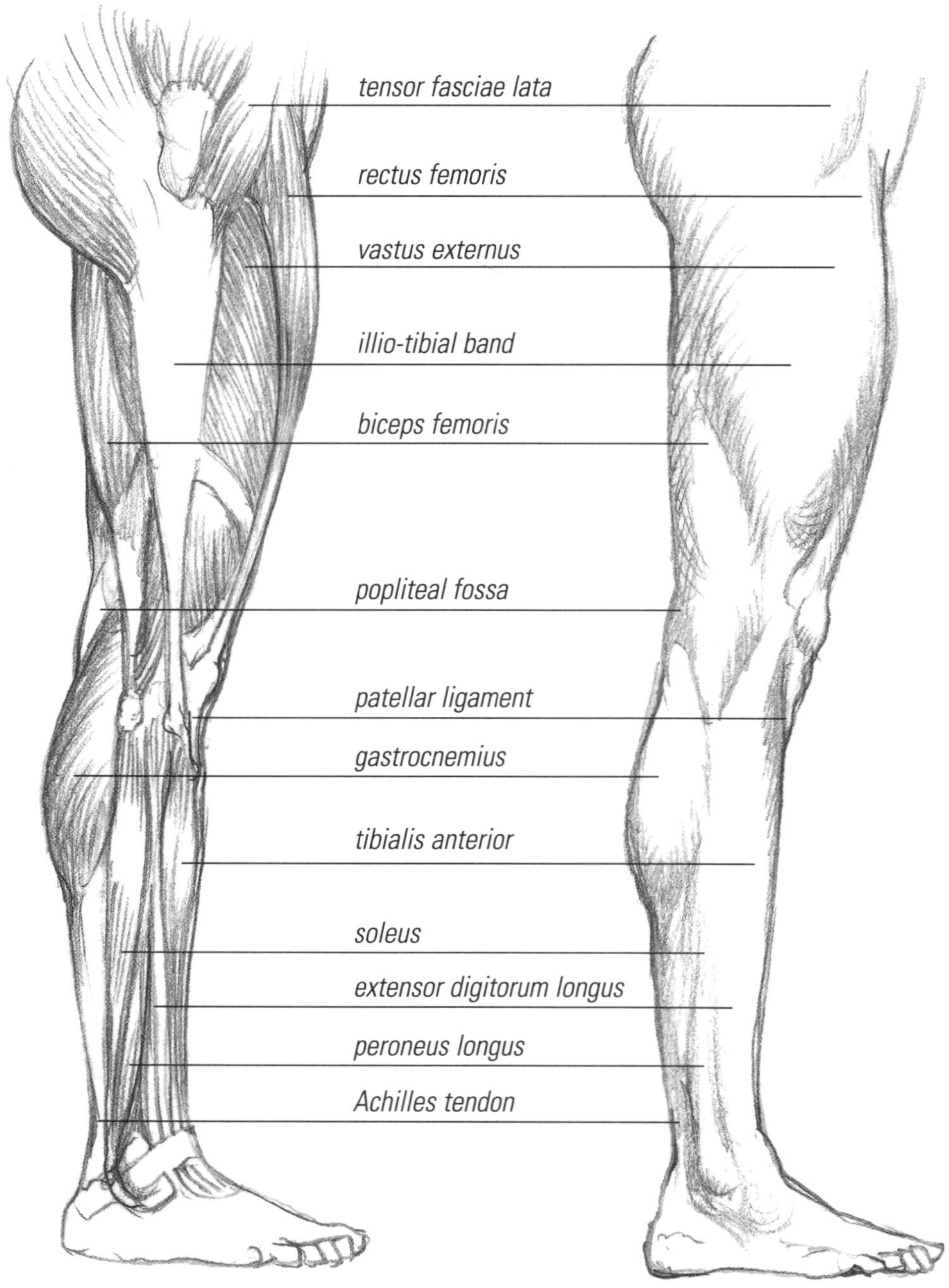

tensor fasciae lata

rectus femoris

vastus externus

illio-tibial band

biceps femoris

popliteal fossa

patellar ligament

gastrocnemius

tibialis anterior

soleus

extensor digitorum longus

peroneus longus

Achilles tendon

Bones and Muscles Because the long *femur* (B), and large *tibia* (H) carry the weight of the body, they sit directly on top of one another. But in a side-view drawing, the upper and lower leg appear staggered; the front of the shin lines up directly below the *illio-tibial band* muscles and behind the upper-leg masses of the *rectus femoris* and *vastus externus*.

In the lower leg, the forms to look for are the *gastrocnemius;* the long, straight form of the *Achilles tendon;* the *peroneus longus* tendon, which passes behind the *outer malleolus* (I) and the bulk of the *extensor digitorum longus;* and the *tibialis anterior,* toward the front of the leg.

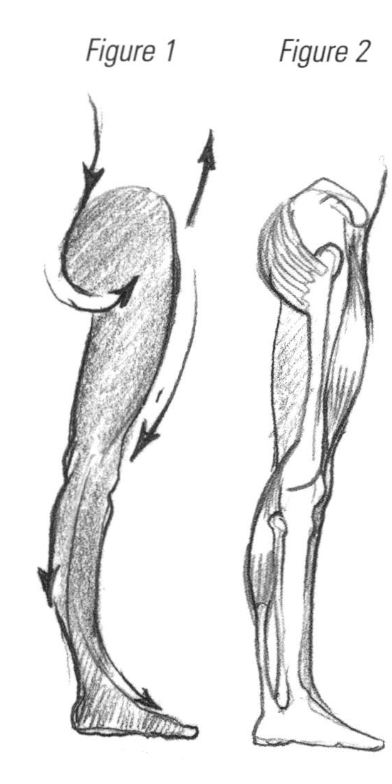

Figure 1   *Figure 2*

Drawing Tips The six arrows in figure 1 show the overall gesture of the leg. The upper thigh and lower calf create the gesture. (See figure 2.) Figure 3 shows the pattern of tendons in the foot. (See page 19.)

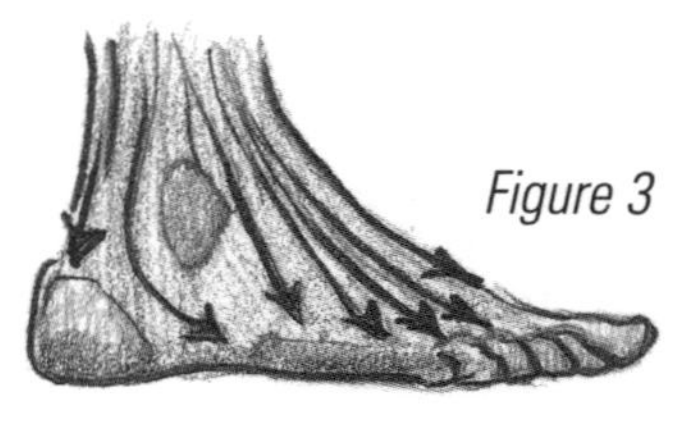

Figure 3

Drawing the Foot

TOP

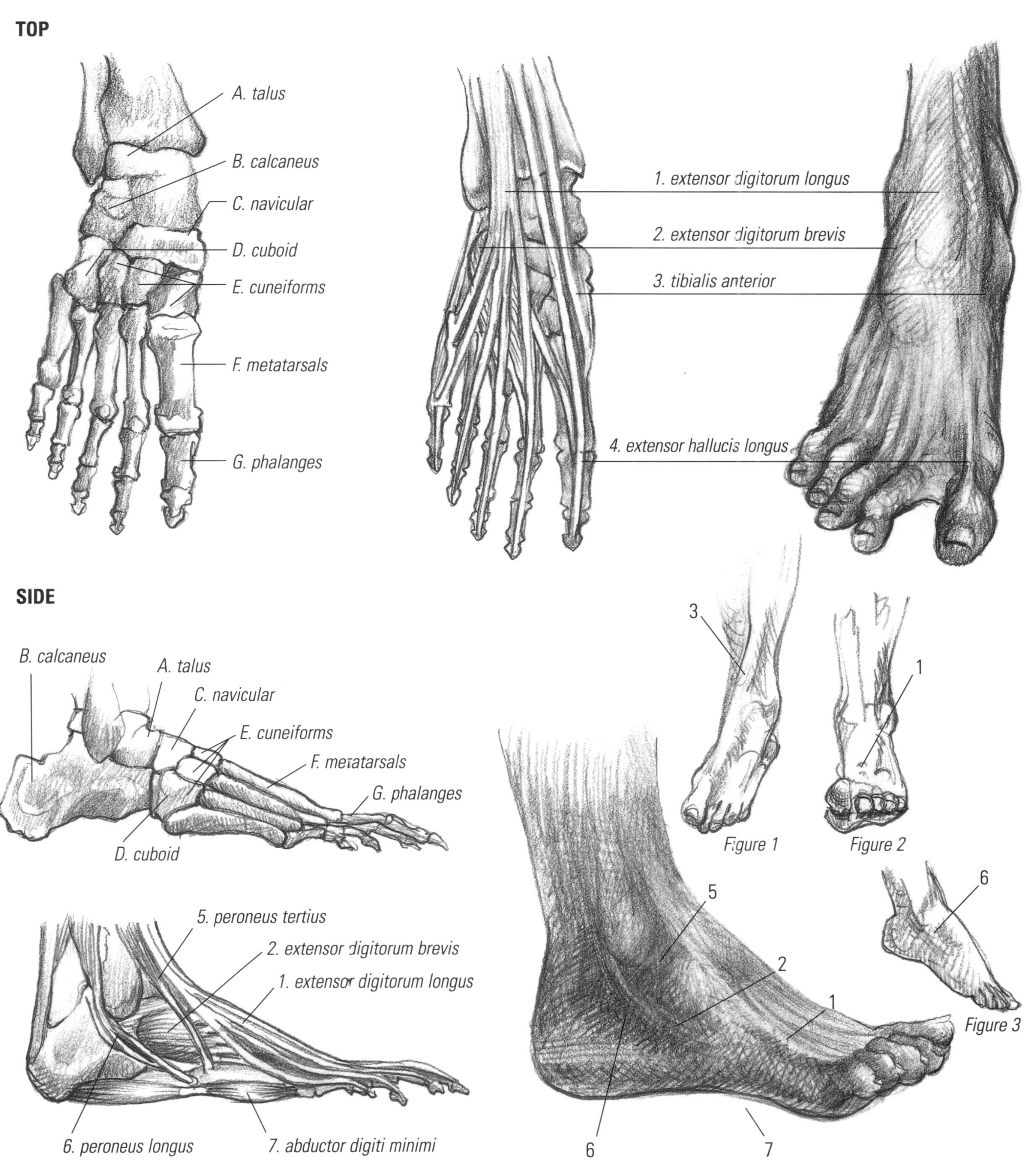

SIDE

Bones Like the hand, the foot also comprises three parts: seven *tarsal* bones (A–E), five *metatarsals* (F), and fourteen *phalanges* (G). The *tarsal* bones include the ankle, heel, and instep. The *metatarsals* are longer and stronger than the five *metacarpals* of the hand, and they end at the ball of the foot. The *phalanges* of the toes are shorter than those of the fingers and thumb; the four small toes press and grip the ground surface, and the big toe tends to have a slight upward thrust.

Muscles When the foot is flexed upward, these tendons are evident: *extensor digitorum longus* (1), *extensor digitorum brevis* (2), *tibialis anterior* (3), and *extensor hallucis longus* (4). (From the side view, *extensor digitorum brevis* appears as a round shape inside a triangular pocket.) *Peroneus longus* (6) curves around the ankle, while *abductor digiti minimi* (7) appears as a bulge on the outer side of the foot.

Drawing Tips The *tibialis anterior* (3) is an obvious landmark on the inverted foot. (See figure 1, above.) In figure 2, dorsi-flexion makes visible the *extensor digitorum* (1). In figure 3, plantar-flexion lets you see the *tendons of peroneus* (6).

Studying the Head and Skull

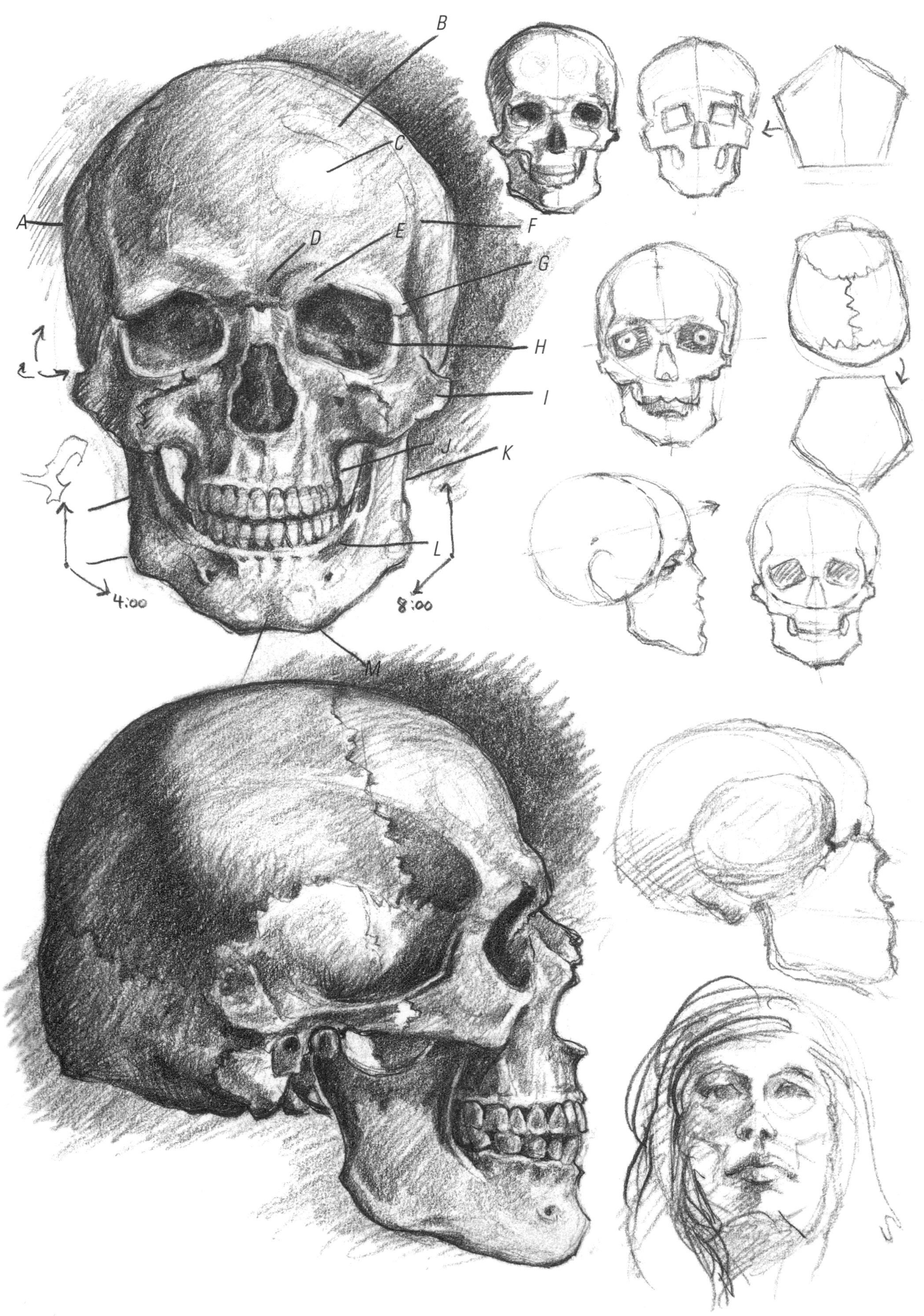

Becoming familiar with the head and skull is an excellent way to improve your portraiture skills. If you purchase a plastic skull, you can practice drawing the skull from all angles, as shown in the charcoal pencil studies above. Start with an outline of the basic shape of the skull; then block in the shapes of the main features and refine the lines (shown in the upper-right corner). The important skull bones for an artist to know are the *parietal eminence* (A), *frontal bone* (B), *frontal eminence* (C), *glabella* (D), *superciliary crest* or "brow ridge" (E), *temporal line* (F), *zygomatic process* (G), *orbit* (H), *zygomatic bone* (I), *maxilla* (J), *ramus of mandible* (K), *mandible* (L), and *mental protuberance* (M).

FRONT VIEW

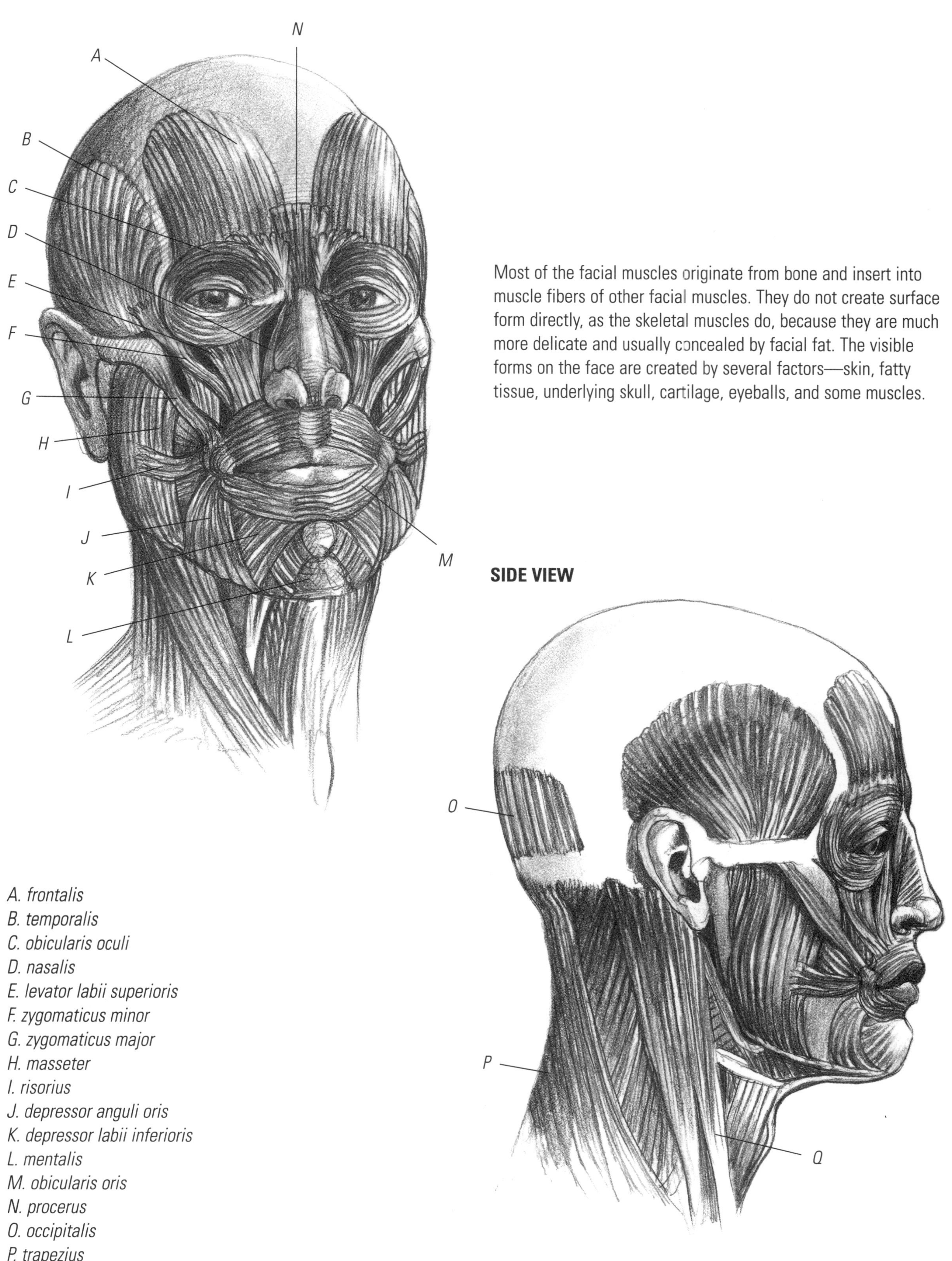

Most of the facial muscles originate from bone and insert into muscle fibers of other facial muscles. They do not create surface form directly, as the skeletal muscles do, because they are much more delicate and usually concealed by facial fat. The visible forms on the face are created by several factors—skin, fatty tissue, underlying skull, cartilage, eyeballs, and some muscles.

A. frontalis
B. temporalis
C. obicularis oculi
D. nasalis
E. levator labii superioris
F. zygomaticus minor
G. zygomaticus major
H. masseter
I. risorius
J. depressor anguli oris
K. depressor labii inferioris
L. mentalis
M. obicularis oris
N. procerus
O. occipitalis
P. trapezius
Q. sternocleidomastoid

FRONT VIEW

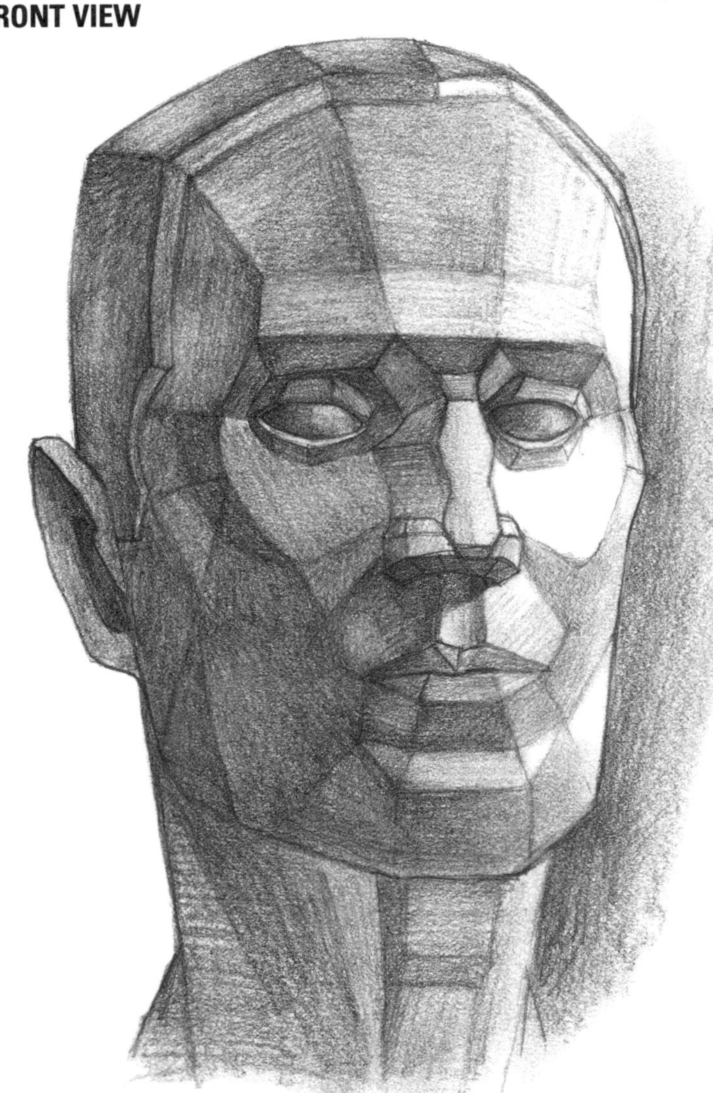

Simplifying the Features When facial muscles contract, they affect the shape of the fatty forms, skin, and other facial muscles, causing the wrinkles, furrows, ridges, and bulges that convey various facial expressions. Simplifying these complex shapes into easily recognizable geometric planes (the "planes of the head") can help guide an artist in the proper placement of light and shadow. As an artist, there's no need to actually sketch the planes, but it helps to understand the planes and visualize them when approaching complex features and shading.

Visualizing Light and Shadow In this final stage, light and shadow are translated from simple planes onto a more subtle, realistic portrait. Self-portraiture is a great way to practice identifying the planes of the head from many different angles. Using a mirror as reference, focus on the placement of the light and dark values that create the form of your face. Just remember to draw what you *really* see in the mirror, not what you *expect* to see.

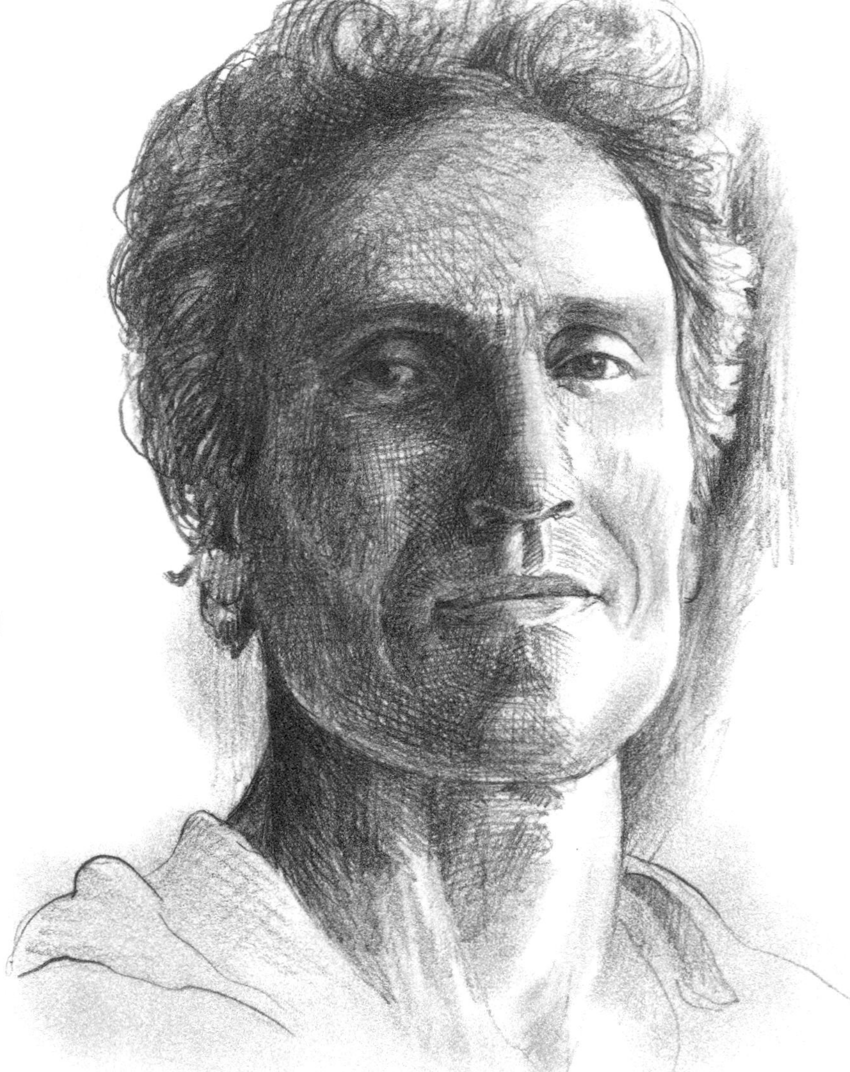

Capturing Facial Features

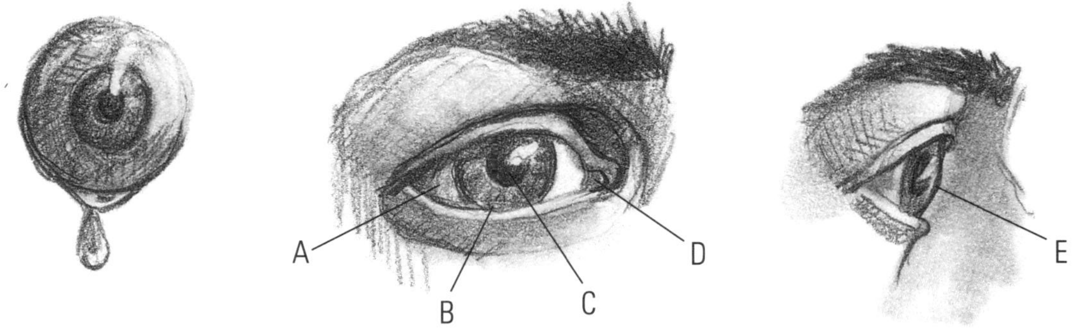

Drawing Tips The *sclera* (A) is the white of the eye. The *iris* (B) is a colored disc that controls the amount of light entering the round opening of the *pupil* (C). The domelike, transparent *cornea* (E) sits over the *iris*. The *inner canthus* (D) at the corner of the eye, is an important feature of the shape of the eye.

The Eye The eyeball is a moist sphere. Because its surface is glossy, the cornea (E) often features a highlight.

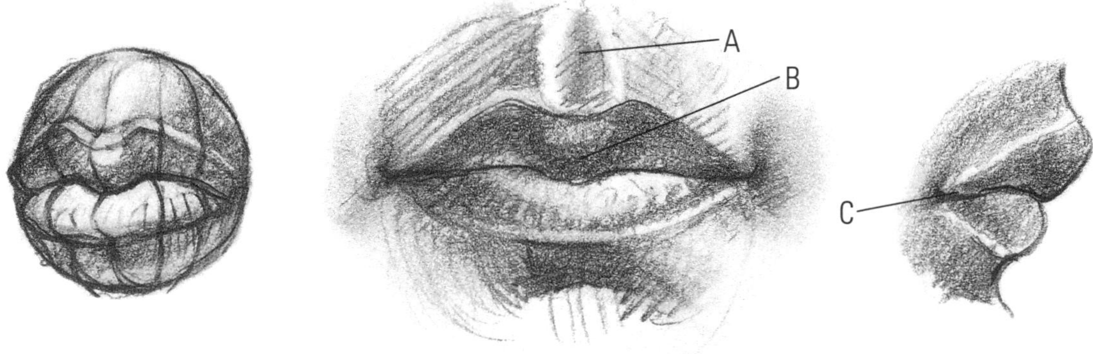

Drawing Tips The vertical furrow between the nose and upper lip is the *philtrum* (A). The *tubercle* (B) of the upper lip is a small rounded form surrounded by two elongated forms; it fits into the middle of the two elongated forms of the lower lip. The *node* (C) is an oval muscular form on the outer edge of the mouth.

The Lips Because the lips curve around the cylinder of the teeth, it's helpful to draw and shade the mouth as if it were a sphere.

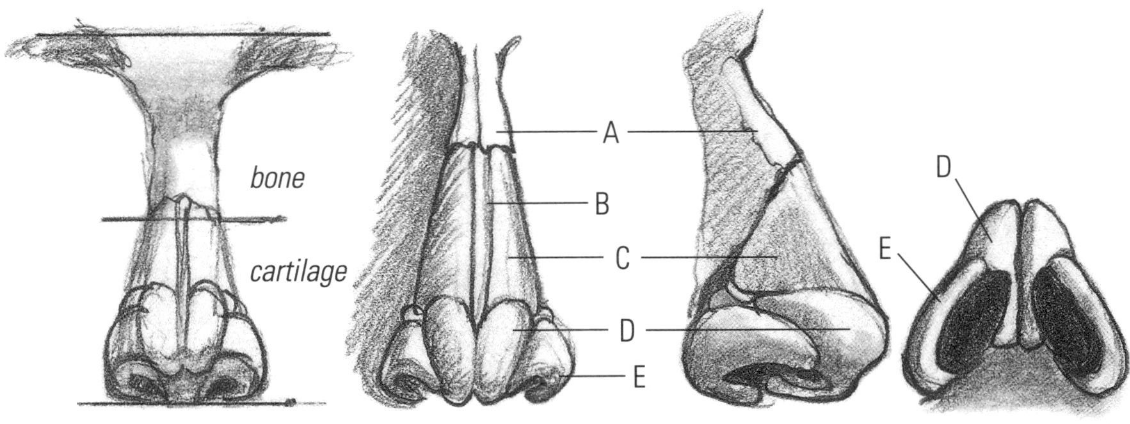

Drawing Tips The bridge of the nose is formed by two *nasal bones* (A). The middle section of the nose is made of a rigid *septal cartilage* (B), surrounded by two *lateral cartilages* (C). The bulb of the nose is formed by two *greater alar cartilages* (D). Two *wings* (E) create the nostrils.

The Nose The nose is made up of bone, cartilage, and fatty tissue. Halfway down from the eyebrows, cartilage replaces the bone.

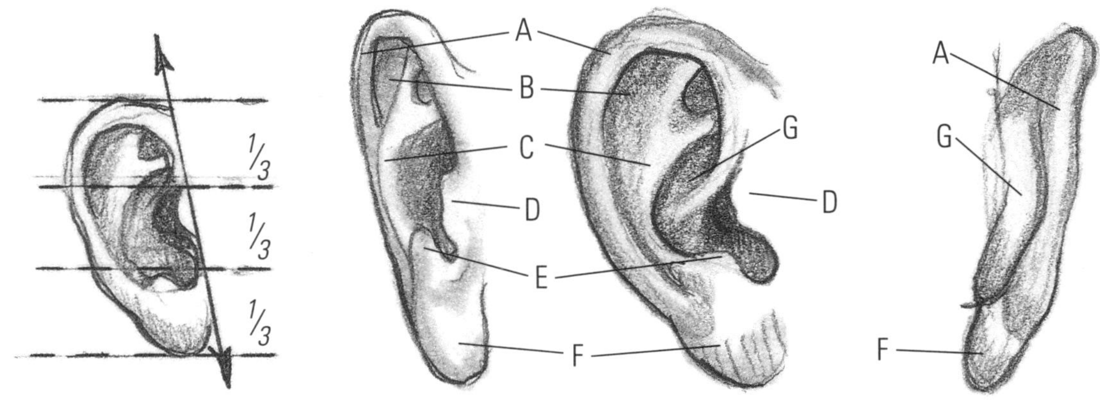

Drawing Tips The cartilaginous *helix* (A) forms the outer rim of the ear. The *antihelix* (C) lies just inside the *helix*, running roughly parallel to it; the two are divided by the *scapha* (B). The *tragus* (D) is a cartilaginous projection, located over the bowl (the *concha*, G). The *antitragus* (E) is located opposite the *tragus* and just above the fatty *lobe* (F).

The Ear Think of the ear as an oval disc divided into three sections and placed on a diagonal angle.

Portraying a Seated Figure in Pencil

Although understanding anatomical theory is an important step for beginning artists, it's equally important to be able to apply that knowledge to your artistic renderings. The figure drawing lessons on pages 24–31 demonstrate applied anatomical theory. Start with a simple pose like this one, which doesn't include the whole body (it excludes the lower legs and feet), and think about the anatomy of the figure while you draw.

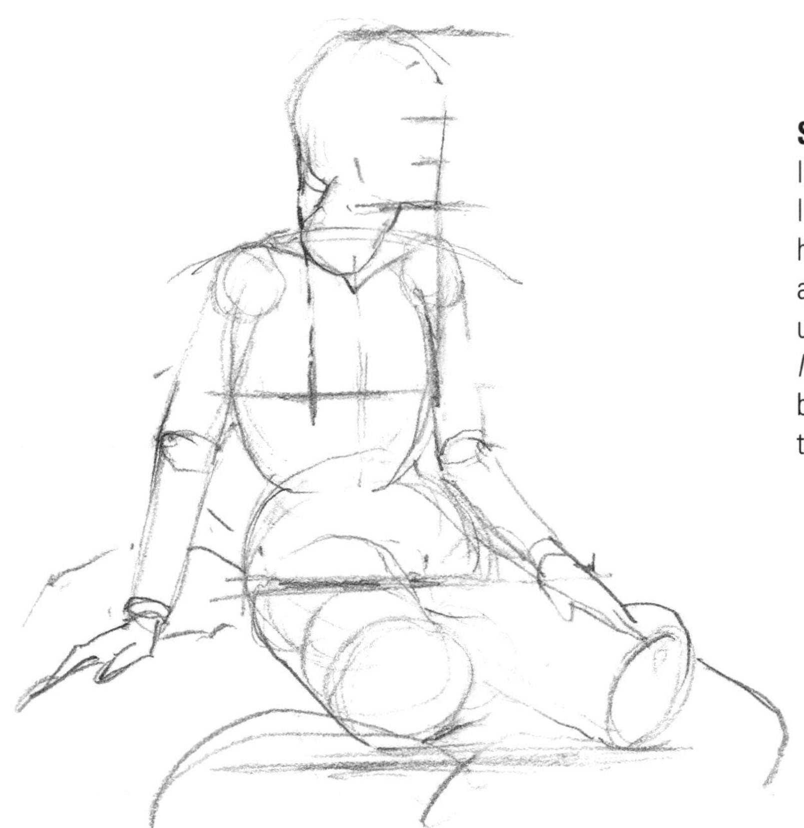

Step One I use the mid-hand position (see page 4) to begin lightly sketching the basic shapes of the subject. First, to establish correct proportions, I divide the figure horizontally into 4 head lengths (see page 6). Then I sketch the rib cage, shoulders, and pelvis as circular forms and establish the arms and legs using cylindrical shapes with straight edges. I also add a *plumb line*—a guideline used to establish vertical alignment—from the back of the head to the right nipple to make sure I don't place the head too far forward or too far back.

Step Two With the framework established, I switch my pencil to a handwriting position to define the anatomical contours. I keep in mind the skeletal and muscular landmarks as I draw, and I vary the strength of my lines to produce both light and dark values, giving the figure a fluid, natural appearance. I pay careful attention to proportions, adding a line from the pit of the neck down the *sternum*—following the *linea alba* through the navel—to establish the vertical center of the torso. Notice that the upper left arm is parallel to this line, and the right arm is at an angle, countering the curve of the body to balance the pose.

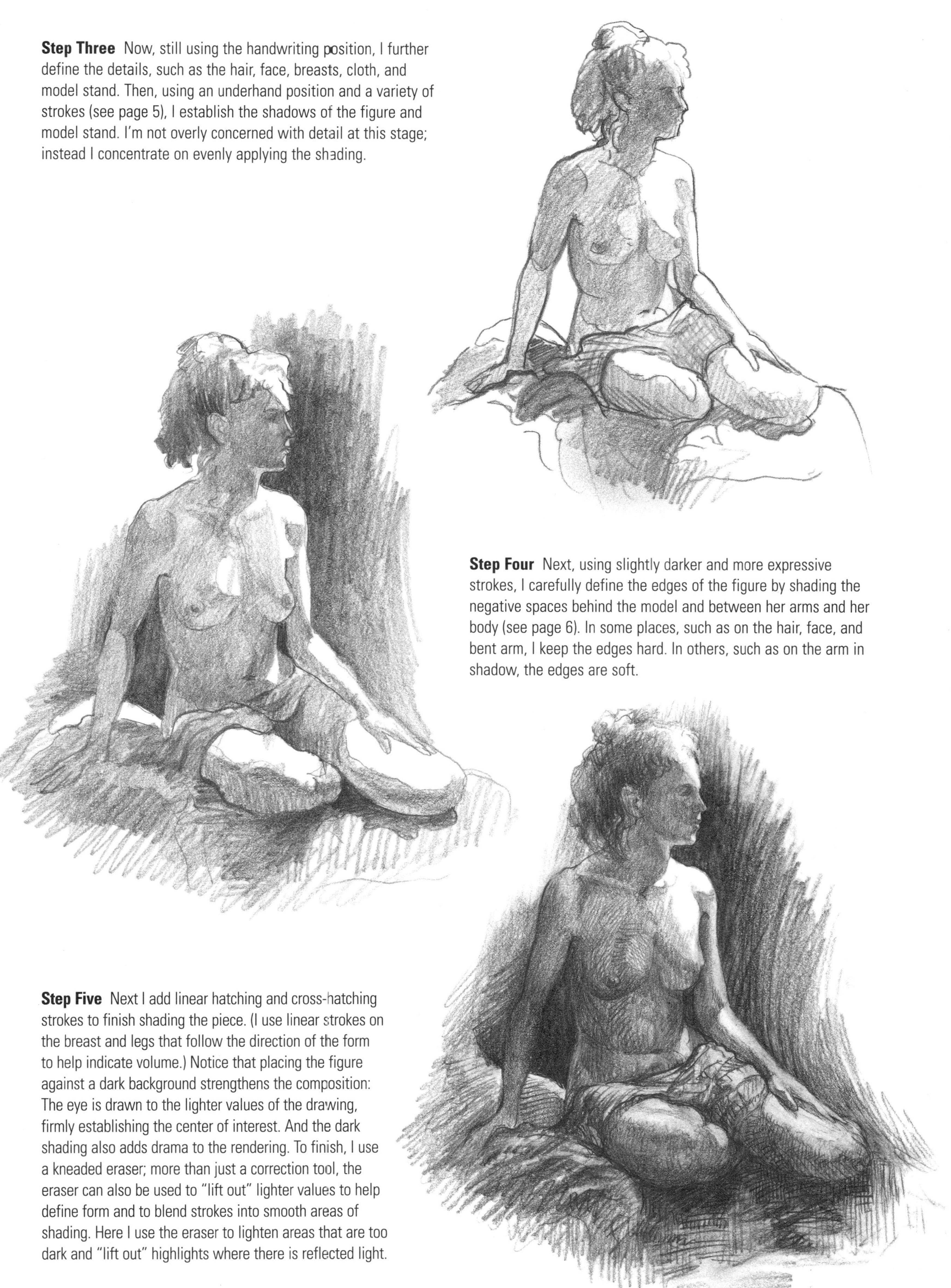

Step Three Now, still using the handwriting position, I further
define the details, such as the hair, face, breasts, cloth, and
model stand. Then, using an underhand position and a variety of
strokes (see page 5), I establish the shadows of the figure and
model stand. I'm not overly concerned with detail at this stage;
instead I concentrate on evenly applying the shading.

Step Four Next, using slightly darker and more expressive
strokes, I carefully define the edges of the figure by shading the
negative spaces behind the model and between her arms and her
body (see page 6). In some places, such as on the hair, face, and
bent arm, I keep the edges hard. In others, such as on the arm in
shadow, the edges are soft.

Step Five Next I add linear hatching and cross-hatching
strokes to finish shading the piece. (I use linear strokes on
the breast and legs that follow the direction of the form
to help indicate volume.) Notice that placing the figure
against a dark background strengthens the composition:
The eye is drawn to the lighter values of the drawing,
firmly establishing the center of interest. And the dark
shading also adds drama to the rendering. To finish, I use
a kneaded eraser; more than just a correction tool, the
eraser can also be used to "lift out" lighter values to help
define form and to blend strokes into smooth areas of
shading. Here I use the eraser to lighten areas that are too
dark and "lift out" highlights where there is reflected light.

Sketching a Standing Figure in Pencil

Many beginning artists prefer to draw figures from a straightforward viewpoint—a good position for practicing anatomical placement and proportion. But what is best for practice is not necessarily best for viewing; the straight-on view is typically too symmetrical to be very compelling. In this composition, the figure is posed rear-forward, providing a fresh and unique perspective. And the figure's pose does not follow a straight line; instead it is curvilinear, with twists and turns that create interest and a turned head that lends drama to the composition. When you develop your own compositions, experiment with different viewpoints until you find the ones that create the most interest.

Step One The easiest way to begin drawing a standing figure is to sketch a simplified figurette. (See page 11.) This sketch is really no more than a glorified stick figure with a head, rib cage, pelvis, and limbs that are represented by simple shapes. The figurette establishes the subject's proportions and alignments.

Step Two Now I convert the flat shapes of the stick figure into geometric ones. (Pick the geometric shape—sphere, cube, cylinder, or pyramid—that most closely resembles each form you are trying to draw.) I also establish several important landmarks, including a line that unites the neck, thorax, and pelvis, running from the *seventh cervicle vertebrae* down the spinal column and ending at the *caudal triangle.*

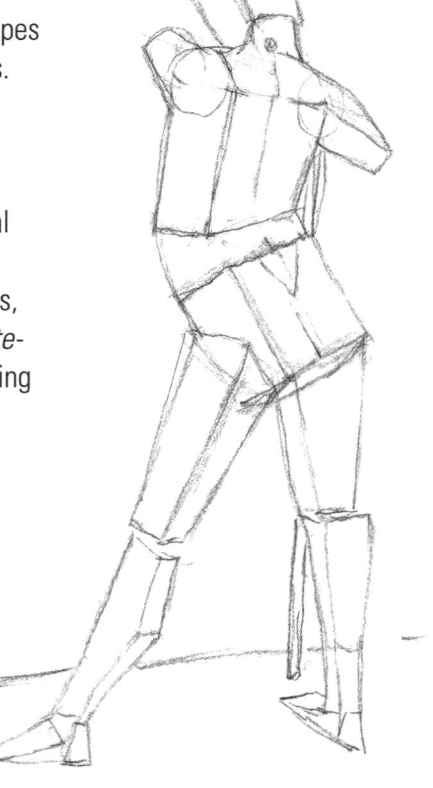

Step Three Just as it is easier to begin a drawing with a long block that resembles a leg than it is to draw an anatomically correct leg, it is easier to simplify shading into light and dark blocks than it is to immediately establish all the nuances of value. This step demonstrates the shading concept, but rather than shading my actual drawing at this stage, I merely block in the placement of the shadows or create a separate study for this purpose. I then use this as a guide for my shading in step four.

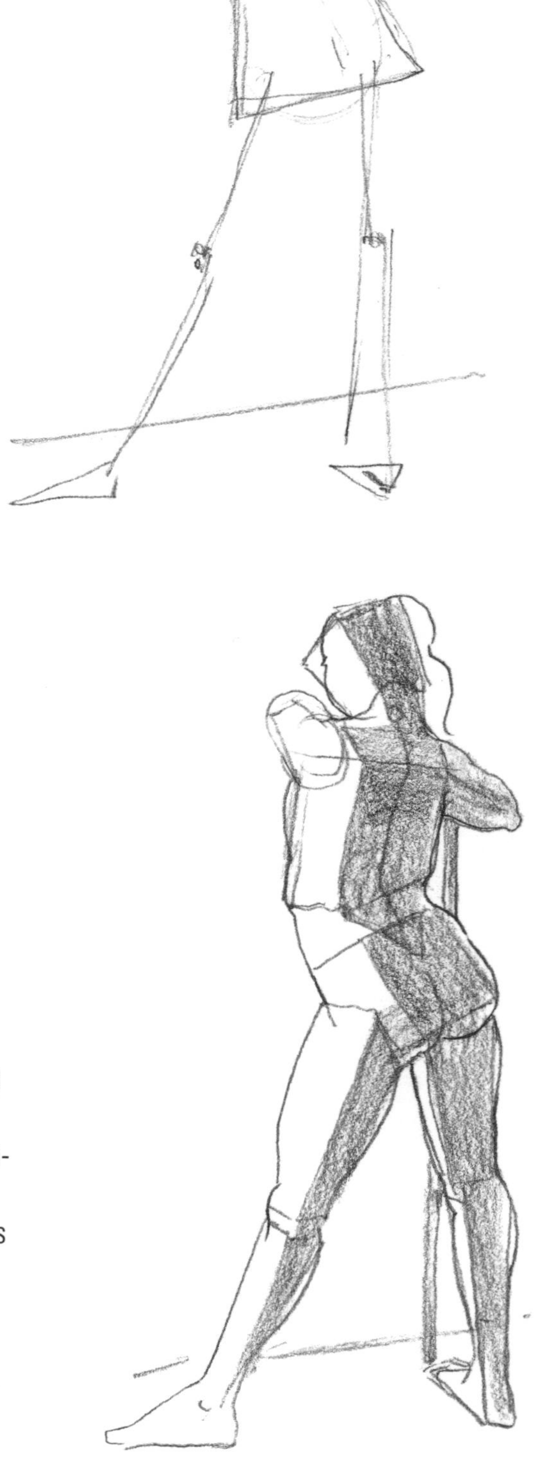

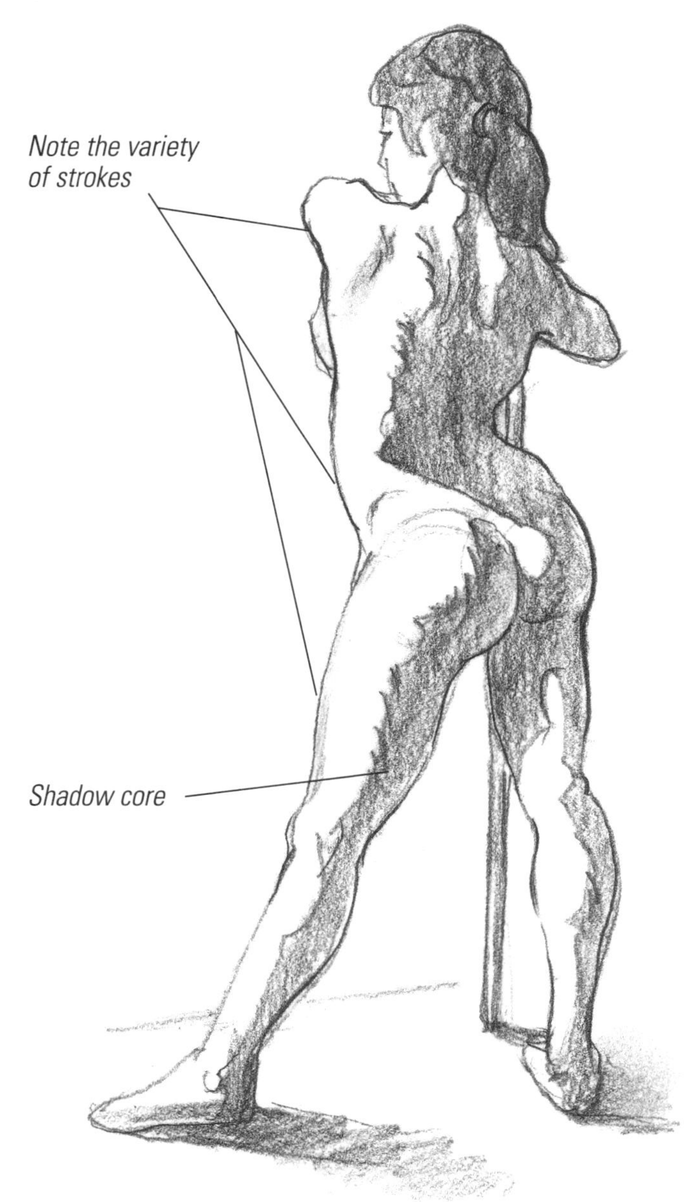

Step Four Holding my pencil in a mid-hand position, I carefully draw the contours of the skeletal landmarks and muscle shapes. I vary the weight of my lines for greater realism and drama, using darker values both to indicate shadows and to emphasize interesting curves. Next, keeping in mind the simplified shading exercise in step three, I draw the shapes of the shadows, filling them with a flat shading stroke. Then I accent the shadow edges (or *shadow cores*) with darker hatched strokes.

Step Five Now I establish the dark tones of the background with varied strokes, butting them up against the figure. This dark shading serves two purposes; it brings forward the illuminated, advancing side of the figure and pushes back the shadowed, receding side. Next I add definition to the drawing: I refine the facial features, add gestural lines to the hair, darken the base of the staff, and accent the shadow cores. To finish, I use a kneaded eraser to pull out very subtle highlights where there is reflected light on the *latissimus dorsi, gluteus medius,* and *adductor group.*

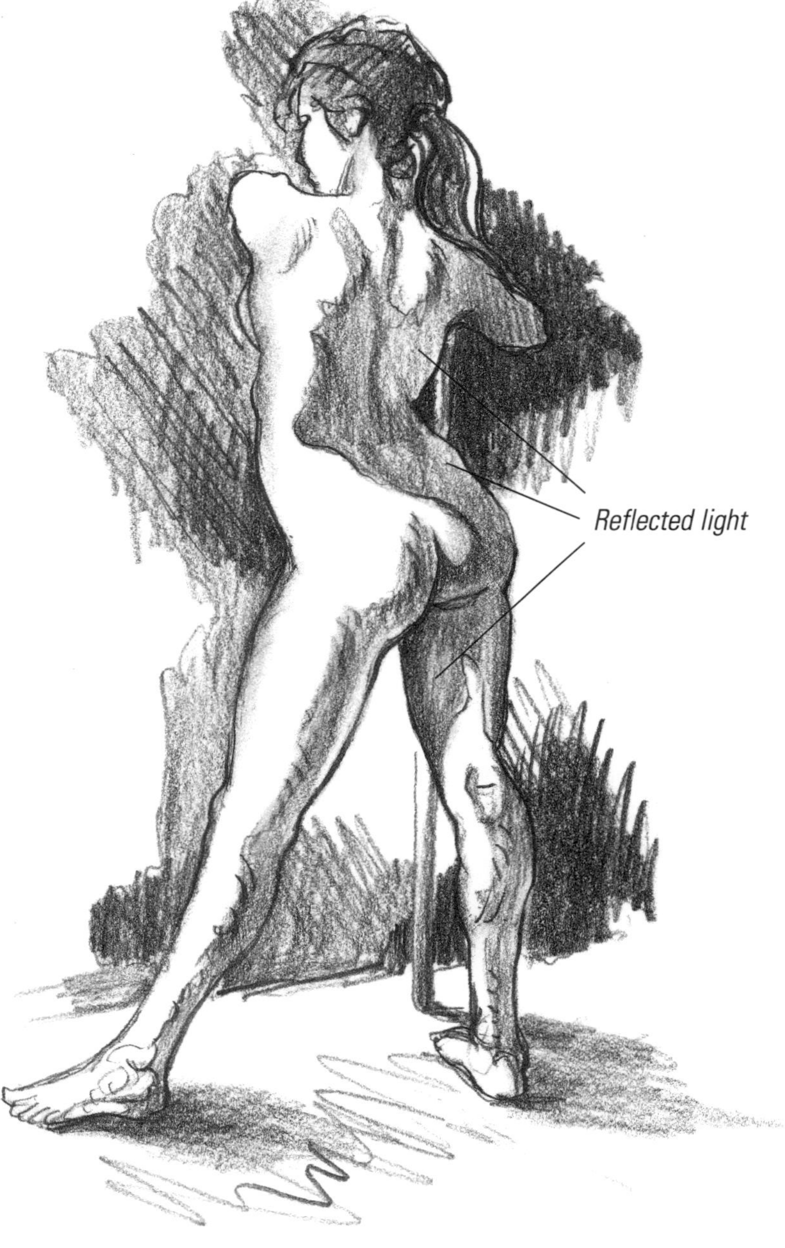

RENDERING A RECLINING FIGURE IN CHARCOAL

Once you've mastered drawing the figure from a simple perspective, try a more complicated pose, such as this reclining figure. Here the body is positioned so that some parts of the body are closer to the viewer than others are, demonstrating foreshortening. *Foreshortening* causes objects to appear larger as they come toward you. When foreshortened, all the same anatomical landmarks are still evident, but their proportions are altered; for example, the length of the calf appears to be shorter than the length of the foot. When you draw figures in foreshortened poses such as this one, disregard the "rules" of proportion and draw the figure as you really see it. Just as the calf appears much shorter than expected, advancing objects also may sometimes appear larger in proportion than you might at first anticipate.

Step One Beginning with a light sketch, I block in the figure's basic angles and outlines with straight lines. (Pay careful attention to the altered proportions you see as you draw.) I use 1 hand length (from finger tip to wrist bone) as my standard unit of measurement for this figure, which is about 4 hands long. As I sketch, I'm careful to check the placement of the anatomical landmarks; for example, I draw a light horizontal line above the buttocks and below the elbow to find the appropriate placements for the shoulder and knee: the shoulder is just below the buttocks and the knee is sightly above the elbow.

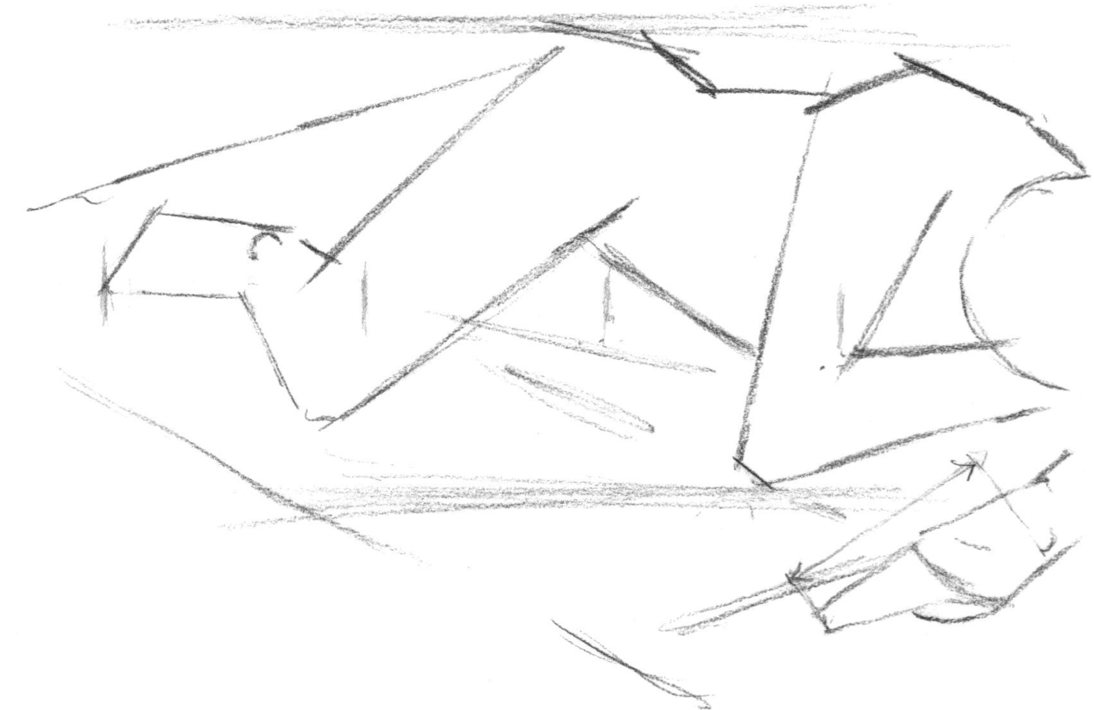

Step Two When I'm pleased with the overall blocking, I begin refining the drawing by giving it dimension. First I create a sphere for the head, and then I convert the limbs and torso into very light cylinders. Because of the foreshortened perspective, the cylinders will appear to either come forward or retreat into the picture's space.

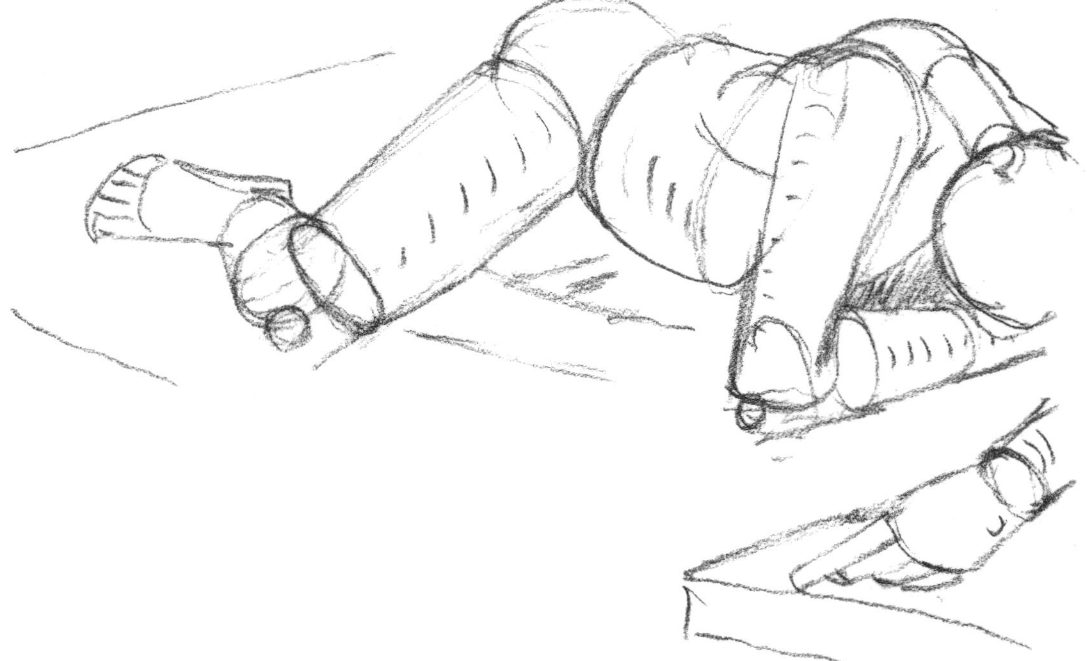

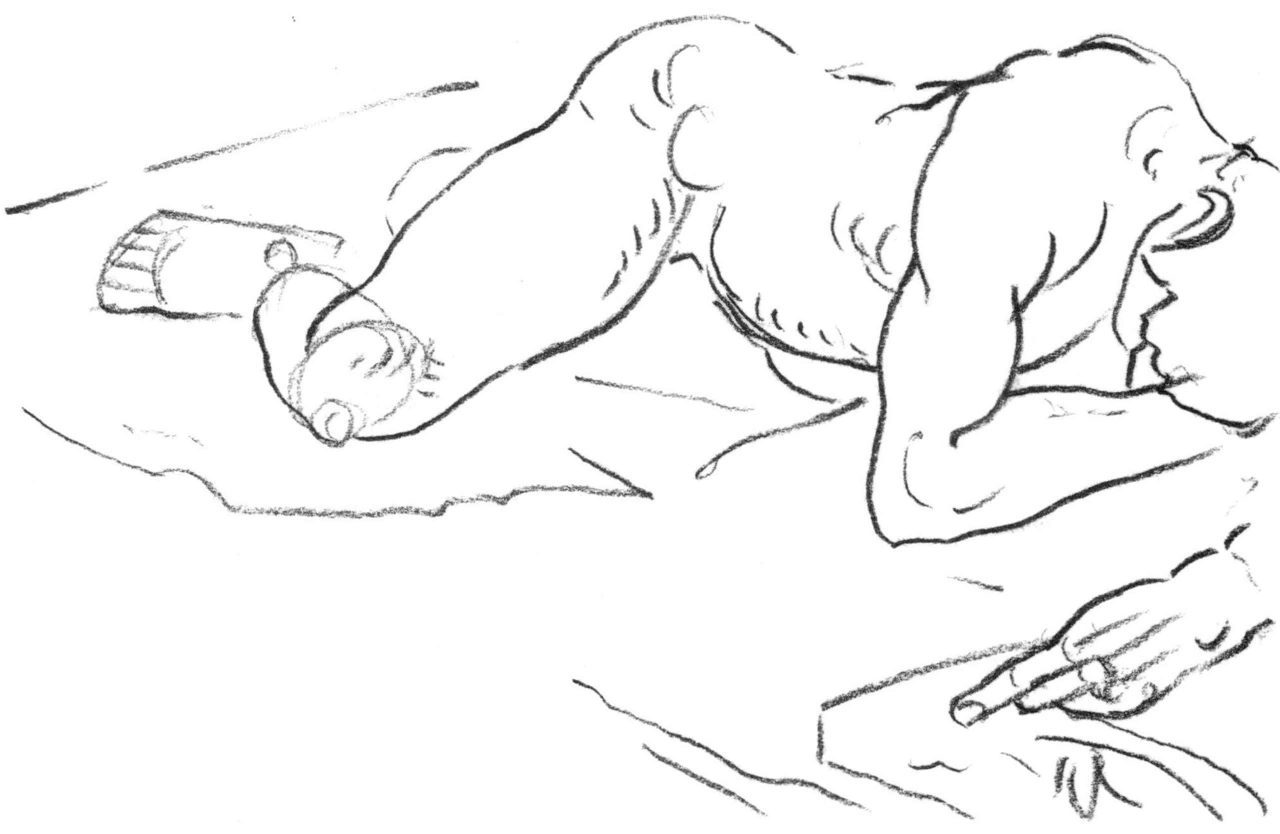

Step Three I check the proportions again before I continue developing my drawing; it is much easier to make any corrections or adjustments at this early stage. Then, using the mid-hand position, I begin defining the actual anatomical contours. This particular pose features many of the prominent bones and muscles covered in this book, such as the *serratus anterior*, evident near the ribs, the *deltoid,* giving shape to the upper arm, and the *outer malleolus,* protruding at the ankle; despite the foreshortening, there are still a good number of readily identifiable landmarks.

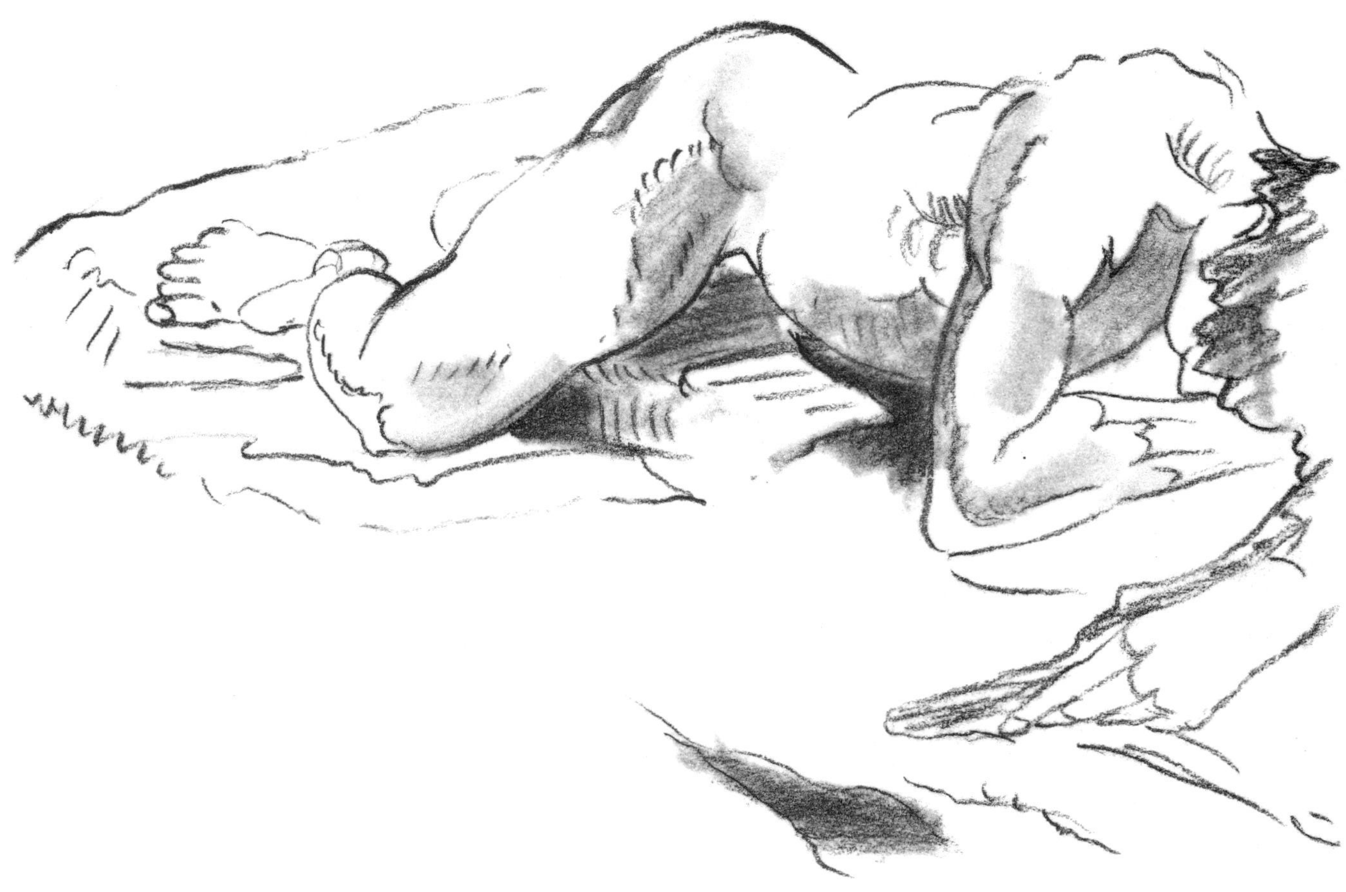

Step Four Now I've established the shape of the contours, but I need to add shading to create dimension and form. Before I begin adding dark values, I carefully analyze the shapes of the shadows and very lightly map out their placement, delineating only the edges of all areas to be shaded. Next I shade inside the areas I've mapped, lightly blocking in a range of values that will serve as a guideline for more detailed shading later.

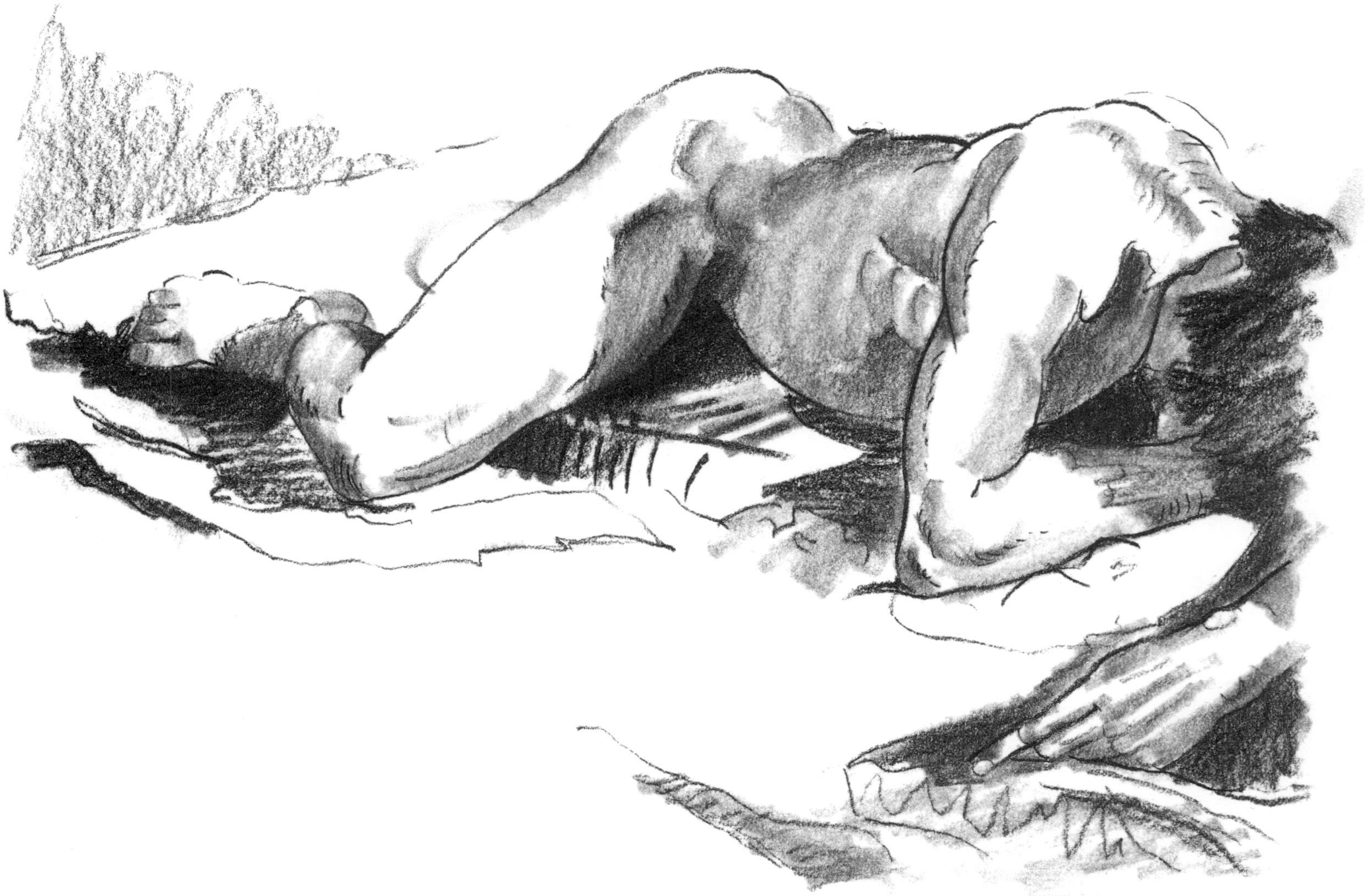

Step Five Next I sharpen my charcoal pencils before I begin the detail work. (Use a pencil sharpener, or see the sharpening techniques on page 3.) With my hand in the underhand position and using smooth, flat strokes, I shade in all the mapped-out shadow areas. It's important to stroke lightly because charcoal gets darker when the strokes are blended. Next I use a stump to blend several midtone areas (A, B, C, and D), and I use a kneaded eraser to lift off the charcoal to create lighter values where I want to indicate tendons (D).

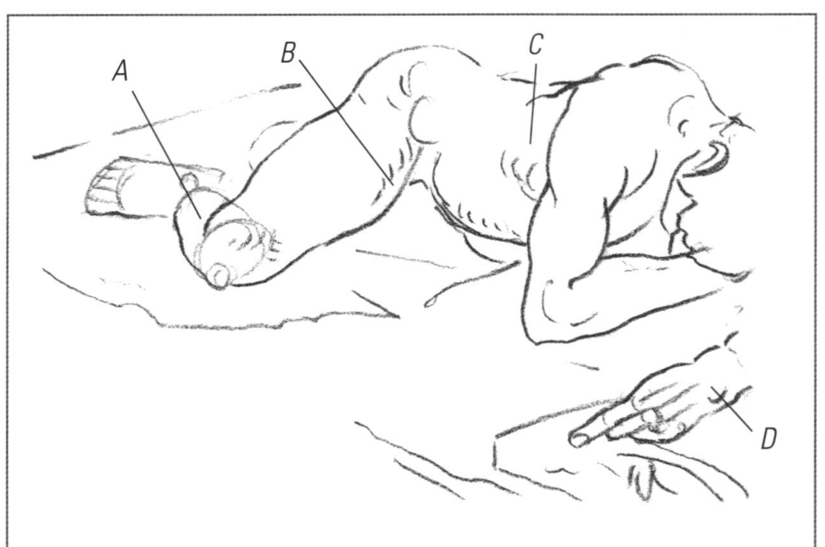

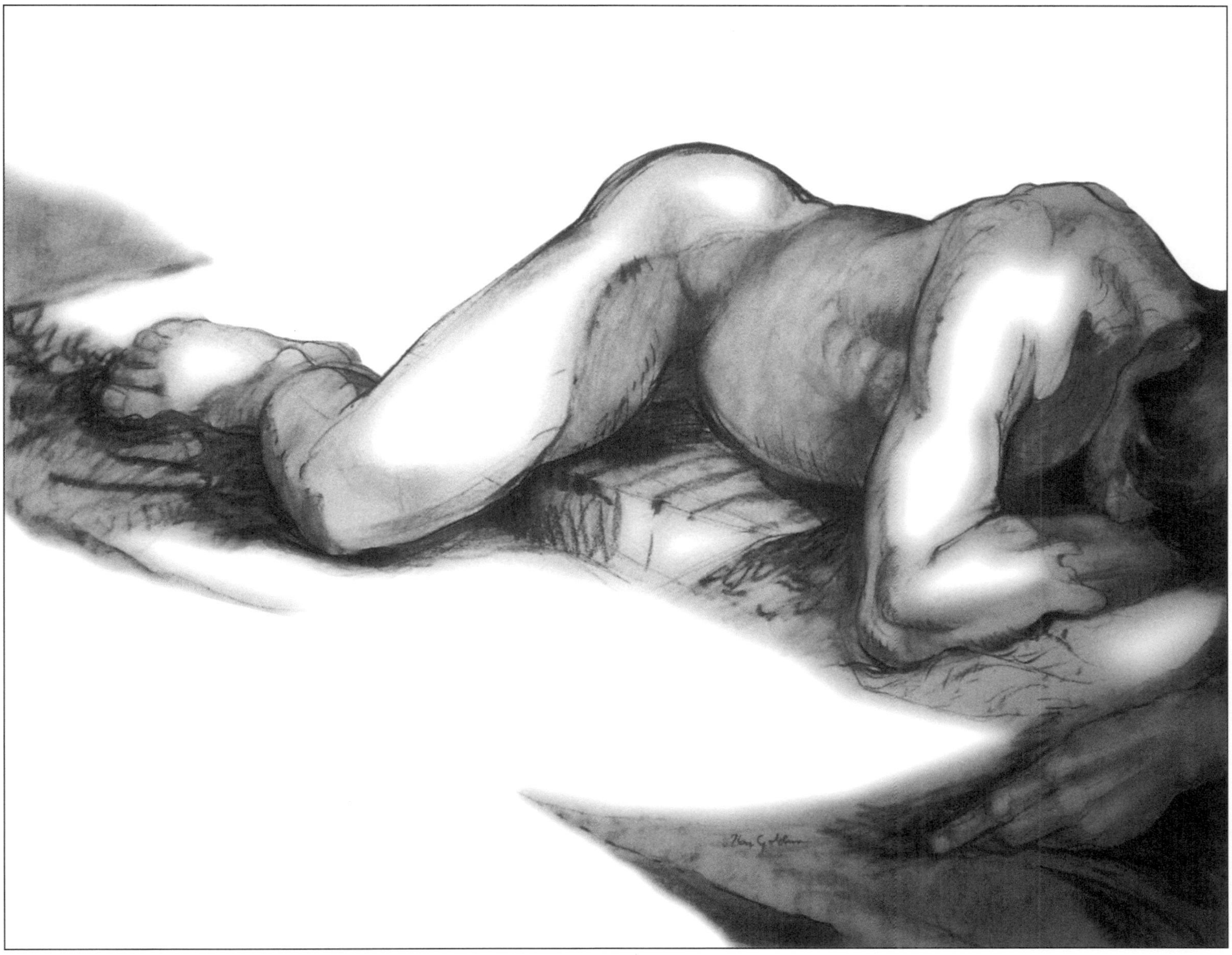

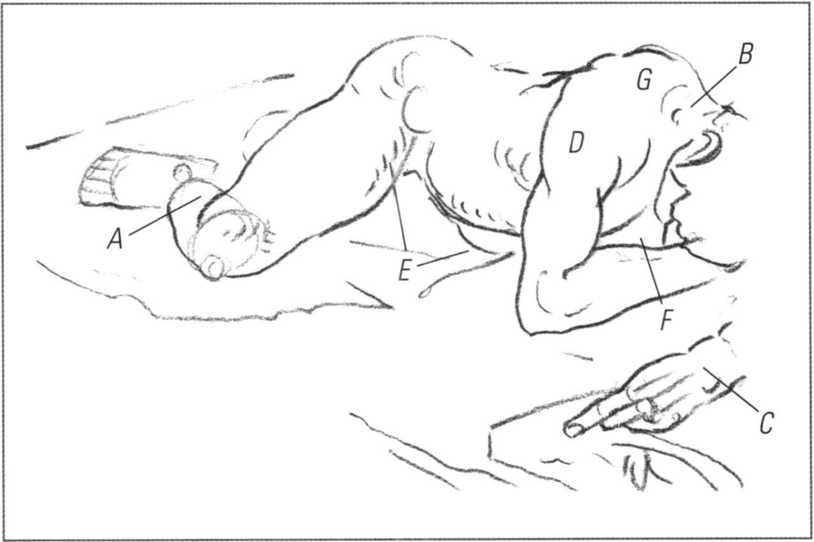

Step Six After I've finished blending, I take a close look at my drawing. I use a kneaded eraser to lighten areas that have become too dark, patiently working back and forth until I am happy with the result. The eraser also helps me achieve the variations in value that are needed to create half-tones (A, B, C), form shadows (D), and cast shadows (E, F). To finish, I add light contour lines to define the shape of the *trapezius* (G), and I accent the *gluteus maximus* with dark lines to liven up the drawing.

Walter Foster Art Instruction Program

THREE EASY STEPS TO LEARNING ART

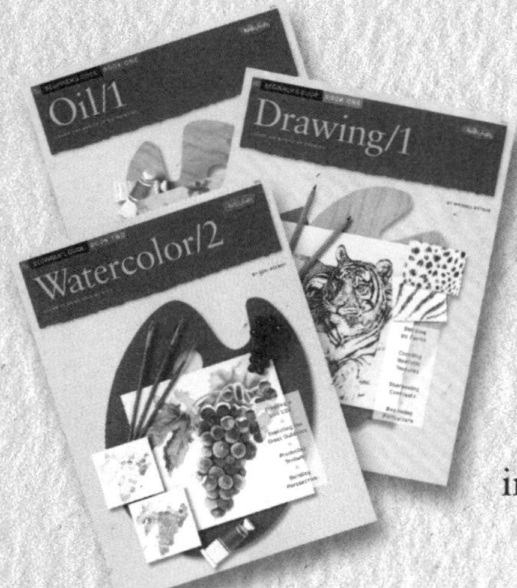

Beginner's Guides are specially written to encourage and motivate aspiring artists. This series introduces the various painting and drawing media—acrylic, oil, pastel, pencil, and watercolor—making it the perfect starting point for beginners. Book One introduces the medium, showing some of its diverse possibilities through beautiful rendered examples and simple explanations, and Book Two instructs with a set of engaging art lessons that follow an easy step-by-step approach.

How to Draw and Paint titles contain progressive visual demonstrations, expert advice, and simple written explanations that assist novice artists through the next stages of learning. In this series, professional artists tap into their experience to walk the reader through the artistic process step by step, from preparation work and preliminary sketches to special techniques and final details. Organized by medium, these books provide insight into an array of subjects.

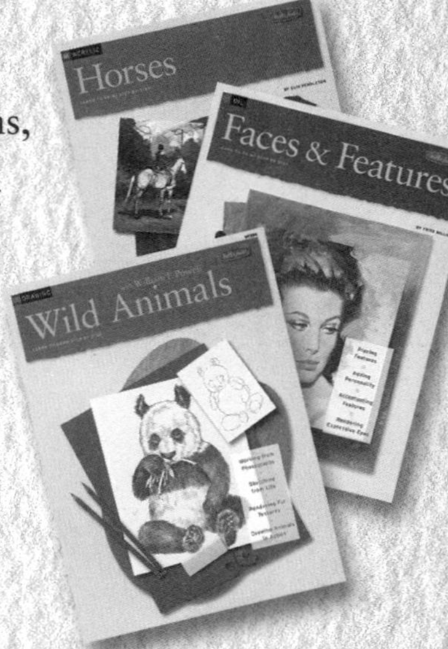

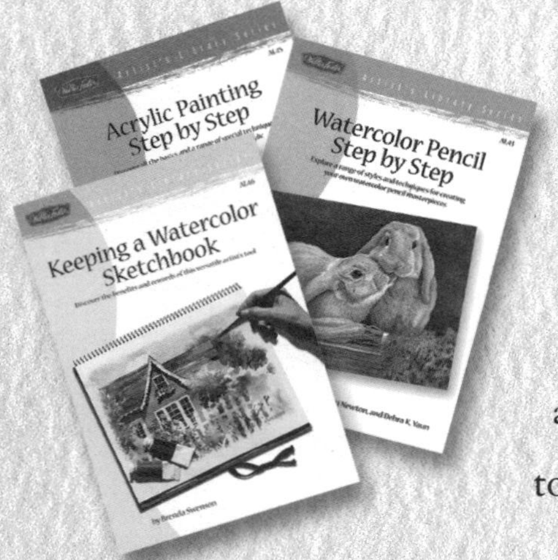

Artist's Library titles offer both beginning and advanced artists the opportunity to expand their creativity, conquer technical obstacles, and explore new media. Written and illustrated by professional artists, the books in this series are ideal for anyone aspiring to reach a new level of expertise. They'll serve as useful tools that artists of all skill levels can refer to again and again.

Walter Foster products are available at art and craft stores everywhere.
For a full list of Walter Foster's titles, visit our website at www.walterfoster.com
or send $5 for a catalog and a $5-off coupon.

WALTER FOSTER PUBLISHING, INC.
23062 La Cadena Drive
Laguna Hills, California 92653
Main Line 949/380-7510
Toll Free 800/426-0099

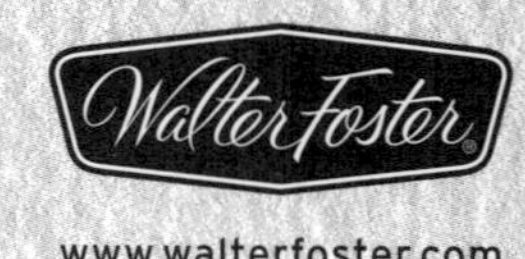

www.walterfoster.com